D0655374

THE
Walker's
Anthology

FURTHER TALES

Compiled by
B R Y N   T H O M A S

TRAILBLAZER PUBLICATIONS

The Walker's Anthology – Further Tales
First edition: 2016

Publisher
Trailblazer Publications
The Old Manse, Tower Rd, Hindhead, Surrey, GU26 6SU, UK
www.trailblazer-guides.com

British Library Cataloguing in Publication Data
A catalogue record for this book is available from the British Library

ISBN 978-1-905864-82-9

Editor: Jane Thomas
Layout: Bryn Thomas
Cover image: 'Seaford', SR poster, 1930
© National Railway Museum / Science & Society Picture Library

Printed on chlorine-free paper by
booksfactory.eu

CONTENTS

INTRODUCTION

'Solvitur ambulando', St Augustine said: 'It is solved by walking'.

Walking is so much more than a means of locomotion, and so much more than a form of physical exercise. Bruce Chatwin writes, 'My God is the God of Walkers. If you walk hard enough, you probably don't need any other god.' For him walking was also a 'poetic activity that can cure the world of all its ills.' Indeed, Wordsworth spent much time walking and it is said that when a visitor asked to see his study, his maid explained, 'Here is his library, but his study is out of doors.'

Philosophers have long agreed that walking is beneficial to thinking. For Jean Jacques Rousseau (see p70) it was crucial: 'Walking animates and enlivens my spirits; I can hardly think when in a state of inactivity; my body must be exercised to make my judgement active.'

Walking can bring freedom in a small way as an escape from the drudgery of everyday life. Written in 1821, *On Going a Journey* by William Hazlitt (see p52), is probably the first piece written specifically on the subject of recreational walking. In his words: 'The soul of a journey is liberty, perfect liberty, to think, feel, do, just as one pleases. We go a journey chiefly to be free of all impediments and of all inconveniences...' But walking can bring freedom of a much more influential kind when it is in the form of a march or demonstration, such as Gandhi's Salt March (see p94).

Our legs can take us to the top of the world (see p100 for Edmund Hillary's account of the last few steps to reach the summit of Everest), or to the ends of the earth – Frank Oates's account of his travels in southern Africa (see p144), Mary Kingsley's in West Africa (p138) and Henry Walter Bates's in Brazil (p125).

Perhaps the best quotation on the subject and importance of walking is that attributed to the Buddha who is said to have given the following advice: 'Above all do not lose your desire to walk... I have walked myself into my best thoughts and know of no thought so burdensome that one cannot walk away from it.'

Keep walking ... and read on for inspiration.

GREAT BRITAIN 1

Seven Sisters, 2015

BILL BRYSON

Twenty years after the publication of his entertaining account of his wanderings round Britain – Notes from a Small Island *– Bryson journeys again through the country that has become his home. His observations of modern Britain are always perceptive and often hilarious as this excerpt from his latest book –* The Road to Little Dribbling *– shows.*

Unnerved by my dossier of stroke warnings, I did some research and it appears that there are two basic ways to avoid having a stroke. One is to die of something else first. The other is to get some exercise. I decided, in the interests of survival, to introduce a little walking into my life. And so it was, the day after my trip from Bognor to Hove, that I was to be found fifteen or so miles to the east wheezing my way up a steep hill to a breezy top called Haven Brow, the first in a series of celebrated eminences gracing the Sussex coast and known as the Seven Sisters.

The Seven Sisters is one of the great walks of England. (They are the hills on the cover of this book, and are a fair size, as you can see.)* From the top of Haven Brow the view is just sensational. Ahead of you stretches a hazy infinity of rolling hills, each ending at the seaward side in a sudden plunge of white chalk. On a sunny day like this one, it is a world of simple, bright elements: green land, white cliffs, deep blue sea, matching sky.

Nothing – and I mean, really, absolutely nothing – is more extraordinary in Britain than the beauty of the countryside. Nowhere in the world is there a landscape that has been more intensively utilized – more mined, farmed, quarried, covered with cities and clanging factories, threaded with motorways and railway lines – and

* Also, coincidentally, on the cover of this anthology.

yet remains so comprehensively and reliably lovely over most of its extent. It is the happiest accident in history. In terms of natural wonders, you know, Britain is a pretty unspectacular place. It has no alpine peaks or broad rift valleys, no mighty gorges or thundering cataracts. It is built to really quite a modest scale. And yet with a few unassuming natural endowments, a great deal of time and an unfailing instinct for improvement, the makers of Britain created the most superlatively park-like landscapes, the most orderly cities, the handsomest provincial towns, the jauntiest seaside resorts, the stateliest homes, the most dreamily spired, cathedral-rich, castle-strewn, abbey-bedecked, folly-scattered, green-wooded, winding-laned, sheep-dotted, plumply hedgerowed, well-tended, sublimely decorated 50,318 square miles the world has ever known – almost none of it undertaken with aesthetics in mind, but all of it adding up to something that is, quite often, perfect. What an achievement that is.

And what a joy it is to walk in it. England and Wales have 130,000 miles of public footpaths, about 2.2 miles of path for every square mile of area. People in Britain don't realize how extraordinary that is. If you told someone in the Midwest of America, where I come from, that you intended to spend the weekend walking across farmland, they would look at you as if you were out of your mind. You couldn't do it anyway. Every field you crossed would end in a barrier of barbed wire. You would find no helpful stiles, no kissing gates, no beckoning wooden footpath posts to guide you on your way. All you would get would be a farmer with a shotgun wondering what the hell you were doing blundering around in his alfalfa.

So if there is one thing I enjoy and admire in Britain, it is the pleasure of being on foot and at large in the open air. I was on the South Downs Way, which runs for a hundred miles from Winchester to Eastbourne along the rolling chalk downs of the south coast. I have done most of the trail in chunks over the years, but this is my favourite stretch. To my left were bosomy hills of green and gold, to the right a spangled plane of bright blue sea. Dividing the two were cliffs of brilliant white. You can, if you dare, creep right up to the cliff edge and look over. Generally you

Every twenty minutes on the Appalachian Trail, Katz and I walked farther than the average American walks in a week.

find a straight drop down two hundred feet to a rocky beach. But almost no one ever does this. It's too unnerving and way too dangerous. These cliff edges are crumbly, so everyone keeps well back. Even frolicking dogs brake and retreat when they see the fall. All along this stretch of coast the path is a grassy lawn, cropped by sheep, sometimes hundreds of yards wide, so even the most absent-minded walker the sort of person who can't be trusted around automated parking barriers, say – can amble along in a state of blissful unawareness and remain safe.

The South Downs Way is not only lovely but getting better. At Birling Gap, roughly halfway between the start of the Seven Sisters and Eastbourne, there used to be a fairly horrible café, but the National Trust has absorbed it into its tasteful care and converted it into a paradise for people who look as if they have just stepped out of a Barbour catalogue. Now there is a smart cafeteria full of scrubbed wooden tables and lovely sea views.

(From *The Road to Little Dribbling – More Notes from a Small Island;* Doubleday, Transworld, London, 2015, © Bill Bryson)

Walking, 1660

THOMAS TRAHERNE

The only way to fully experience the environment is to walk, as Thomas Traherne (1637-74) points out.

> To walk abroad is, not with eyes,
> But thoughts, the fields to see and prize;
> Else may the silent feet,
> Like logs of wood,
> Move up and down, and see no good
> Nor joy nor glory meet.
>
> Ev'n carts and wheels their place do change,
> But cannot see, though very strange
> The glory that is by;
> Dead puppets may
> Move in the bright and glorious day,
> Yet not behold the sky.

. . . . **Four times I was honked at for having the temerity to proceed through town without the benefit of metal.**

BILL BRYSON *A WALK IN THE WOODS*

And are not men than they more blind,
Who having eyes yet never find
The bliss in which they move;
Like statues dead
They up and down are carried
Yet never see nor love.

To walk is by a thought to go;
To move in spirit to and fro;
To mind the good we see;
To taste the sweet;
Observing all the things we meet
How choice and rich they be.

To note the beauty of the day,
And golden fields of corn survey;
Admire each pretty flow'r
With its sweet smell;
To praise their Maker, and to tell
The marks of his great pow'r.

To fly abroad like active bees,
Among the hedges and the trees,
To cull the dew that lies
On ev'ry blade,
From ev'ry blossom; till we lade
Our minds, as they their thighs.

Observe those rich and glorious things,
The rivers, meadows, woods, and springs,
The fructifying sun;
To note from far
The rising of each twinkling star
For us his race to run.

A little child these well perceives,
Who, tumbling in green grass and leaves,
May rich as kings be thought,
But there's a sight

There is scarcely any writer who has not celebrated the happiness of rural privacy, and delighted himself and his reader

Which perfect manhood may delight,
To which we shall be brought.

While in those pleasant paths we talk,
'Tis that tow'rds which at last we walk;
For we may by degrees
Wisely proceed
Pleasures of love and praise to heed,
From viewing herbs and trees.

(From *The Poetical Works of Thomas Traherne*; Dobell, London, 1903)

Walking at Grasmere, 1800

DOROTHY WORDSWORTH

Sunday, 27th June, 1800. – After tea we rowed down to Loughrigg Fell, visited the white foxglove, gathered wild straw-berries, and walked up to view Rydale. We lay a long time look-ing at the lake; the shores all dim with the scorching sun. The ferns were turning yellow, that is here and there one was quite turned. We walked round by Benson's wood home. The lake was now most still, and reflected the beautiful yellow and blue and purple and grey colours of the sky. We heard a strange sound in the Bainriggs wood, as we were floating on the water; it *seemed* in the wood, but it must have been above it, for presently we saw a raven very high above us. It called out, and the dome of the sky seemed to echo the sound. It called again and again as it flew onwards, and the mountains gave back the sound, seeming as if from their centre; a musical bell-like answering to the bird's hoarse voice. We heard both the call of the bird, and the echo, after we could see him no longer.

Friday Evening, 29th August, 1800. – We walked over the hill by the firgrove. I sate upon a rock, and observed a flight of swallows gathering together high above my head. They flew towards Rydale. We walked through the wood over the stepping-stones. The lake of Rydale very beautiful, partly still. John and I left Wm. to compose an inscription; that about the path. We had a very fine

with the melody of birds, the whisper of groves, and the mur-mur of rivulets. SAMUEL JOHNSON

walk by the gloomy lake. There was a curious yellow reflection in the water, as of corn fields. There was no light in the clouds from which it appeared to come.

Saturday Morning, 30th August. –... William finished his Inscription of the Pathway, then walked in the wood; and when John returned, he sought him, and they bathed together. I read a little of Boswell's *Life of Johnson*. I went to lie down in the orchard. I was roused by a shout that Anthony Harrison was come. We sate in the orchard till tea time. Drank tea early, and rowed down the lake, which was stirred by breezes. We looked at Rydale, which was soft, cheerful, and beautiful. We then went to peep into Langdale. The Pikes were very grand. We walked back to the view of Rydale, which was now a dark mirror. We rowed home over a lake still as glass, and then went to George Mackareth's to hire a horse for John. A fine moonlight night. The beauty of the moon was startling, as it rose to us over Loughrigg Fell. We returned to supper at 10 o'clock.

(From *Journals*, 1800)

On Elizabeth Bennet, 1813

JANE AUSTEN

Caroline Bingley and her sister Louisa Hurst do not consider it proper for Elizabeth Bennet to have walked the three miles to Netherfield rather than coming in a carriage. Caroline's brother and his friend Mr Darcy are rather less critical...

Her manners were pronounced to be very bad indeed, a mixture of pride and impertinence; she had no conversation, no style, no beauty. Mrs. Hurst thought the same, and added:

'She has nothing, in short, to recommend her, but being an excellent walker. I shall never forget her appearance this morning. She really looked almost wild.'

'She did, indeed, Louisa. I could hardly keep my countenance. Very nonsensical to come at all! Why must she be scampering about the country, because her sister had a cold? Her hair, so untidy, so blowsy!'

When I walk with you I feel as if I had a flower in my buttonhole.
WILLIAM MAKEPEACE THACKERAY

'Yes, and her petticoat; I hope you saw her petticoat, six inches deep in mud, I am absolutely certain; and the gown which had been let down to hide it not doing its office.'

'Your picture may be very exact, Louisa,' said Bingley; 'but this was all lost upon me. I thought Miss Elizabeth Bennet looked remarkably well when she came into the room this morning. Her dirty petticoat quite escaped my notice.'

'You observed it, Mr. Darcy, I am sure,' said Miss Bingley; 'and I am inclined to think that you would not wish to see your sister make such an exhibition.'

'Certainly not.'

'To walk three miles, or four miles, or five miles, or whatever it is, above her ankles in dirt, and alone, quite alone! What could she mean by it? It seems to me to show an abominable sort of conceited independence, a most country-town indifference to decorum.'

'It shows an affection for her sister that is very pleasing,' said Bingley.

'I am afraid, Mr. Darcy,' observed Miss Bingley in a half whisper, 'that this adventure has rather affected your admiration of her fine eyes.'

'Not at all,' he replied; 'they were brightened by the exercise.'

(From *Pride and Prejudice*; T. Egerton, London, 1813)

Night Walk through London, 1860
CHARLES DICKENS

Owing to his insomnia Dickens would often spend much of the night out walking. Reading his descriptions of his London wanderings one can clearly see where he found the inspiration for some of the characters and scenes in his books.

Some years ago, a temporary inability to sleep, referable to a distressing impression, caused me to walk about the streets all night, for a series of several nights. The disorder might have taken a long time to conquer, if it had been faintly experimented on in bed; but, it was soon defeated by the brisk treatment of getting up

If I could not walk far and fast, I think I should just explode and perish. CHARLES DICKENS

directly after lying down, and going out, and coming home tired at sunrise.

In the course of those nights, I finished my education in a fair amateur experience of houselessness. My principal object being to get through the night, the pursuit of it brought me into sympathetic relations with people who have no other object every night in the year.

The month was March, and the weather damp, cloudy, and cold. The sun not rising before half-past five, the night perspective looked sufficiently long at half-past twelve: which was about my time for confronting it.

The restlessness of a great city, and the way in which it tumbles and tosses before it can get to sleep, formed one of the first entertainments offered to the contemplation of us houseless people. It lasted about two hours. We lost a great deal of companionship when the late public-houses turned their lamps out, and when the potmen thrust the last brawling drunkards into the street; but stray vehicles and stray people were left us, after that. If we were very lucky, a policeman's rattle sprang and a fray turned up; but, in general, surprisingly little of this diversion was provided. Except in the Haymarket, which is the worst kept part of London, and about Kent-street in the Borough, and along a portion of the line of the Old Kent-road, the peace was seldom violently broken. But, it was always the case that London, as if in imitation of individual citizens belonging to it, had expiring fits and starts of restlessness. After all seemed quiet, if one cab rattled by, half-a-dozen would surely follow; and Houselessness even observed that intoxicated people appeared to be magnetically attracted towards each other; so that we knew when we saw one drunken object staggering against the shutters of a shop, that another drunken object would stagger up before five minutes were out, to fraternise or fight with it.

☆　☆　☆

Walking the streets under the pattering rain, Houselessness would walk and walk and walk, seeing nothing but the interminable tangle of streets, save at a corner, here and there, two

Nothing like a night time stroll to give you ideas.
J.K. ROWLING

policemen in conversation, or the sergeant or inspector looking after his men. Now and then in the night – but rarely – Houselessness would become aware of a furtive head peering out of a doorway a few yards before him, and, coming up with the head, would find a man standing bolt upright to keep within the doorway's shadow, and evidently intent upon no particular service to society. Under a kind of fascination, and in a ghostly silence suitable to the time, Houselessness and this gentleman would eye one another from head to foot, and so, without exchange of speech, part, mutually suspicious. Drip, drip, drip, from ledge and coping, splash from pipes and water-spouts, and by-and-by the houseless shadow would fall upon the stones that pave the way to Waterloo-bridge; it being in the houseless mind to have a halfpenny worth of excuse for saying 'Good-night' to the toll-keeper, and catching a glimpse of his fire.

... I chose next to wander by Bethlehem Hospital; partly, because it lay on my road round to Westminster; partly, because I had a night fancy in my head which could be best pursued within sight of its walls and dome. And the fancy was this: Are not the sane and the insane equal at night as the sane lie a dreaming? Are not all of us outside this hospital, who dream, more or less in the condition of those inside it, every night of our lives? Are we not nightly persuaded, as they daily are, that we associate preposterously with kings and queens, emperors and empresses, and notabilities of all sorts? Do we not nightly jumble events and personages and times and places, as these do daily? Are we not sometimes troubled by our own sleeping inconsistencies, and do we not vexedly try to account for them or excuse them, just as these do sometimes in respect of their waking delusions? Said an afflicted man to me, when I was last in a hospital like this, 'Sir, I can frequently fly.' I was half ashamed to reflect that so could I – by night.

Once – it was after leaving the Abbey and turning my face north – I came to the great steps of St. Martin's church as the clock

It is not easy to walk alone in the country without musing upon something. CHARLES DICKENS

was striking Three. Suddenly, a thing that in a moment more I should have trodden upon without seeing, rose up at my feet with a cry of loneliness and houselessness, struck out of it by the bell, the like of which I never heard. We then stood face to face looking at one another, frightened by one another. The creature was like a beetle-browed hair-lipped youth of twenty, and it had a loose bundle of rags on, which it held together with one of its hands. It shivered from head to foot, and its teeth chattered, and as it stared at me – persecutor, devil, ghost, whatever it thought me – it made with its whining mouth as if it were snapping at me, like a worried dog. Intending to give this ugly object money, I put out my hand to stay it – for it recoiled as it whined and snapped – and laid my hand upon its shoulder. Instantly, it twisted out of its garment, like the young man in the New Testament, and left me standing alone with its rags in my hands.

☆   ☆   ☆

Covent-garden Market, when it was market morning, was wonderful company. The great waggons of cabbages, with grow-ers' men and boys lying asleep under them, and with sharp dogs from market-garden neighbourhoods looking after the whole, were as good as a party. But one of the worst night sights I know in London, is to be found in the children who prowl about this place; who sleep in the baskets, fight for the offal, dart at any object they think they can lay their thieving hands on, dive under the carts and barrows, dodge the constables, and are perpetually making a blunt pattering on the pavement of the Piazza with the rain of their naked feet. A painful and unnatural result comes of the comparison one is forced to institute between the growth of corruption as displayed in the so much improved and cared for fruits of the earth, and the growth of corruption as displayed in these all uncared for (except inasmuch as ever-hunted) savages.

There was early coffee to be got about Covent-garden Market, and that was more company – warm company, too, which was better. Toast of a very substantial quality, was like-wise procurable: though the towzled-headed man who made it, in an inner chamber within the coffee-room, hadn't got his coat

I have two doctors, my left leg and my right.
G.M. TREVELYAN

on yet, and was so heavy with sleep that in every interval of toast and coffee he went off anew behind the partition into complicated cross-roads of choke and snore, and lost his way directly.

Into one of these establishments (among the earliest) near Bow-street, there came one morning as I sat over my houseless cup, pondering where to go next, a man in a high and long snuff-coloured coat, and shoes, and, to the best of my belief, nothing else but a hat, who took out of his hat a large cold meat pudding; a meat pudding so large that it was a very tight fit, and brought the lining of the hat out with it. This mysterious man was known by his pudding, for on his entering, the man of sleep brought him a pint of hot tea, a small loaf, and a large knife and fork and plate. Left to himself in his box, he stood the pudding on the bare table, and, instead of cutting it, stabbed it, overhand, with the knife, like a mortal enemy; then took the knife out, wiped it on his sleeve, tore the pudding asunder with his fingers, and ate it all up. The remembrance of this man with the pudding remains with me as the remembrance of the most spectral person my houselessness encountered. Twice only was I in that establishment, and twice I saw him stalk in (as I should say, just out of bed, and presently going back to bed), take out his pudding, stab his pudding, wipe the dagger, and eat his pudding all up. He was a man whose figure promised cadaverousness, but who had an excessively red face, though shaped like a horse's. On the second occasion of my seeing him, he said huskily to the man of sleep, 'Am I red to-night?' 'You are,' he uncompromisingly answered. 'My mother,' said the spectre, 'was a red-faced woman that liked drink, and I looked at her hard when she laid in her coffin, and I took the complexion.' Somehow, the pudding seemed an unwholesome pudding after that, and I put myself in its way no more.

(From *The Uncommercial Traveller*, 1861)

Walking is man's best medicine.
HIPPOCRATES

Inappropriate conversations with Mr Mybug, 1932
STELLA GIBBONS

Mr Meyerburg (nicknamed Mr Mybug) is a writer pursuing Flora with amorous intentions. He has only one thing on his mind.

It cannot be said that Flora really enjoyed taking walks with Mr. Mybug. To begin with, he was not really interested in anything but sex. This was understandable, if deplorable. After all, many of our best minds have had the same weakness. The trouble about Mr. Mybug was that ordinary objects, which are not usually associated with sex even by our best minds, did·suggest sex to Mr. Mybug, and he pointed them out and made comparisons and asked Flora what she thought about it all. Flora found it difficult to reply because she was not interested. She was therefore obliged merely to be polite, and Mr. Mybug mistook her lack of enthusiasm and thought it was due to inhibitions. He remarked how curious it was that most Englishwomen (most young Englishwomen, that was, Englishwomen of about nineteen to twenty-four) were inhibited. Cold, that was what young Englishwomen from nineteen to twenty-four were.

They used sometimes to walk through a pleasant wood of young birch trees which were just beginning to come into bud. The stems reminded Mr. Mybug of phallic symbols and the buds made Mr. Mybug think of nipples and virgins. Mr. Mybug pointed out to Flora that he and she were walking on seeds which were germinating in the womb of the earth. He said it made him feel as if he were trampling on the body of a great brown woman. He felt as if he were a partner in some mighty rite of gestation.

Flora used sometimes to ask him the name of a tree, but he never knew.

Yet there were occasions when he was not reminded of a pair of large breasts by the distant hills. Then, he would stand looking at the woods upon the horizon. He would wrinkle up his eyes and breathe deeply through his nostrils and say that the view reminded him of one of Poussin's lovely things. Or he would peer in a pool and say it was like a painting by Manet ...

The world is mud-luscious and puddle-wonderful.
e.e. CUMMINGS

God! that little pool down there in the hollow was shaped just like somebody's navel. He would like to drag off his clothes and leap into it. There was another problem ... We should have to tackle that, too. In no other country but England was there so much pruriency about nakedness. If we all went about naked, sexual desire would automatically disappear. Had Flora ever been to a party where everybody took off all their clothes? Mr. Mybug had. Once a whole lot of us bathed in the river with nothing on and afterwards little Harriet Belmont sat naked in the grass and played to us on her flute. It was delicious; so gay and simple and natural. And Billie Polswelt danced a Haiwaian love-dance, making all the gestures that are usually omitted in the stage version. Her husband had danced too. It had been lovely; so warm and natural and *real*, somehow.

So, taking it all round, Flora was pleased to have her walk in solitude.

(From *Cold Comfort Farm*; Longmans, 1932, © Stella Gibbons)

The Naturalist's Summer-Evening Walk, 1769

Gilbert White

Gilbert White (1720-93) was a pioneering naturalist and regarded as the first ecologist in the country. His Natural History of Selborne *(1789), the village in Hampshire where he was also the curate, is still in print. The book mainly comprises a collection of letters written to the zoologist Thomas Pennant and to Daines Barrington, a barrister. Sometimes, as here, White writes in verse but ever the naturalist he cannot resist including numerous footnotes to add more about the birds or their habits mentioned in the poem.*

To Thomas Pennant, Esquire

The Naturalist's Summer-evening Walk

… equidem credo, quia sit divinitus illis Ingenium. Virg. Georg.

When day declining sheds a milder gleam,
What time the may-fly[1] haunts the pool or stream;
When the still owl skims round the grassy mead,

It was easier to think if I was walking.
Ernest Hemmingway

What time the timorous hare limps forth to feed;
Then be the time to steal adown the vale,
And listen to the vagrant² cuckoo's tale,
To hear the clamorous³ curlew call his mate,
Or the soft quail his tender pain relate;
To see the swallow sweep the dark'ning plain
Belated, to support her infant train;
To mark the swift in rapid giddy ring
Dash round the steeple, unsubdu'd of wing:
Amusive birds! – say where your hid retreat
When the frost rages and the tempests beat;
Whence your return, by such nice instinct led,
When spring, soft season, lifts her bloomy head?
Such baffled searches mock man's prying pride,
The God of Nature is your secret guide!
While deep'ning shades obscure the face of day
To yonder bench, leaf-shelter'd, let us stray,
Till blended objects fail the swimming sight,
And all the fading landscape sinks in night;
To hear the drowsy dorr come brushing by
With buzzing wing, or the shrill⁴ cricket cry;
To see the feeding bat glance through the wood;
To catch the distant falling of the flood;
While o'er the cliff th' awakened churn-owl hung
Through the still gloom protracts his chattering song;
While high in air, and pois'd upon his wings,
Unseen, the soft enamour'd woodlark⁵ sings:
These, Nature's works, the curious mind employ,
Inspire a soothing melancholy joy:
As fancy warms, a pleasing kind of pain
Steals o'er the cheek, and thrills the creeping vein!
Each rural sight, each sound, each smell combine;
The tinkling sheep-bell, or the breath of kine;
The new-mown hay that scents the swelling breeze,
Or cottage-chimney smoking through the trees.
The chilling night-dews fall: away, retire;
For see, the glow-worm lights her amorous fire!⁶

**Any man that walks the mead
In bud, or blade, or bloom, may find
A meaning suited to his mind.** LORD TENNYSON

Thus, ere night's veil had half obscured the sky,
Th' impatient damsel hung her lamp on high:
True to the signal, by love's meteor led,
Leander hasten'd to his Hero's bed.[7]

[1] The angler's may-fly, the *ephemera vulgata* Linn., comes forth from its aurelia state, and emerges out of the water about six in the evening, and dies about eleven at night, determining the date of its fly state in about five or six hours. They usually begin to appear about the 4th of June, and continue in succession for near a fortnight. See Swammerdam, Derham, Scopoli, etc.

[2] Vagrant cuckoo; so called because, being tied down by no incubation or attendance about the nutrition of its young, it wanders without control.

[3] *Charadrius aedicnemus.*

[4] *Gryllus campestris.*

[5] In hot summer nights woodlarks soar to a prodigious height, and hang singing in the air.

[6] The light of the female glow-worm (as she often crawls up the stalk of a grass to make herself more conspicuous) is a signal to the male, which is a slender dusky scarabaeus.

[7] See the story of Hero and Leander.

(From *The Natural History of Selborne*; T. Bensley for B. White & Son, London, 1789)

Preparations for a long walk, 1933
PATRICK LEIGH FERMOR

After various setbacks at several schools and then being unable to settle down to writing, eighteen-year-old Leigh Fermor resolves to 'change scenery; abandon London and England and set out across Europe like a tramp – or, as I characteristically phrased it to myself, like a pilgrim or palmer, an errant scholar'. Gripped by the idea he prepares quickly and departs in the middle of winter.

During the last days, my outfit assembled fast. Most of it came from Millet's army surplus store in the Strand: an old Army greatcoat, different layers of jersey, grey flannel shirts, a couple of white linen ones for best, a soft leather windbreaker, puttees, nailed boots, a sleeping bag (to be lost within a month and neither missed nor replaced); notebooks and drawing blocks, rubbers, an aluminium cylinder full of Venus and Golden Sovereign pencils; an old *Oxford Book of English Verse*. (Lost likewise, and,

Of all exercises walking is the best.
THOMAS JEFFERSON

to my surprise – it had been a sort of Bible – not missed much more than the sleeping bag.) The other half of my very conventional travelling library was the Loeb *Horace*, Vol. I, which my mother, after asking what I wanted, had bought and posted in Guildford. (She had written the translation of a short poem by Petronius on the flyleaf, chanced on and copied out, she told me later, from another volume on the same shelf: 'Leave thy home, O youth, and seek out alien shores ... Yield not to misfortune: the far-off Danube shall know thee, the cold North-wind and the untroubled kingdom of Canopus and the men who gaze on the new birth of Phoebus or upon his setting...' She was an enormous reader, but Petronius was not in her usual line of country and he had only recently entered mine. I was impressed and touched.) Finally I bought a ticket on a small Dutch steamer sailing from Tower Bridge to the Hook of Holland. All this had taken a shark's bite out of my borrowed cash, but there was still a wad of notes left over.

At last, with a touch of headache from an eve-of-departure party, I got out of bed on the great day, put on my new kit and tramped south-west under a lowering sky. I felt preternaturally light, as though I were already away and floating like a djinn escaped from its flask through the dazzling middle air while Europe unfolded. But the grating hobnails took me no further than Cliveden Place, where I picked up a rucksack left for me there by Mark Ogilvie-Grant. Inspecting my stuff, he had glanced with pity at the one I had bought. (His – a superior Bergen affair resting on a lumbar semicircle of metal and supported by a triangular frame – had accompanied him – usually, he admitted, slung on a mule – all round Athos with Robert Byron and David Talbot-Rice when *The Station* was being written. Weathered and faded by Macedonian suns, it was rife with *mana*.)

Then I bought for ninepence a well-balanced ashplant at the tobacconist's next to the corner of Sloane Square and headed for Victoria Street and Petty France to pick up my new passport. Filling in the form the day before – born in London, 11 February 1915; height 5' 9¾"; eyes, brown; hair, brown; distinguishing marks, none – I had left the top space empty, not knowing what

After dinner sit awhile, after supper walk a mile.
OLD ENGLISH PROVERB

to write. Profession? 'Well, what shall we say?' the passport official had asked, pointing to the void. My mind remained empty. A few years earlier, an American hobo song called 'Hallelujah I'm a bum!' had been on many lips; during the last days it had been haunting me like a private *leitmotif* and without realising I must have been humming the tune as I pondered, for the official laughed. 'You can't very well put *that*, he said. After a moment he added: 'I should just write 'student';' so I did. With the stiff new document in my pocket, stamped '8 December 1933', I struck north over the Green Park under a dark massing of cloud. As I crossed Piccadilly and entered the crooked chasm of White Horse Street, there were a few random splashes and, glistening at the end of it, Shepherd Market was prickly with falling drops. I would be just in time for a goodbye luncheon with Miss Stewart and three friends – two fellow lodgers and a girl: then, away. The rain was settling in.

(From *A Time of Gifts – On Foot to Constantinople: from the Hook of Holland to the Middle Danube; John Murray, London, 1977, © Patrick Leigh Fermor*)

Solvitur Ambulando, 1934

ARTHUR STANLEY

There is nothing more conducive to sleep than fresh air and exercise. If Sleep refuses her gift because during the day you have withheld these offerings, it is never too late to make amends. Don't go to bed just yet, or if already there get up, dress yourself and go out for a short walk. If it be dark, wet and windy, good and well; groping through darkness and battling with wind and rain will make you more fit for sleep. If the moon be shining clearly out of a windless sky, the quiet beauty of the night will give you almost a foretaste of sleep. In any case you will very likely add something notable to your experiences. The night-walker is at least sure of one reward – a comforting feeling of superiority to the 'folk in housen'. Don't go far, don't walk fast, and go to bed at once when you return.

(From *The Bedside Book*, compiled by Arthur Stanley, Victor Gollancz, 1934)

'Solvitur ambulando', St. Augustine said.
'It is solved by walking'.
LAURA KELLY, *DISPATCHES FROM THE REPUBLIC OF OTHERNESS*

Market Day, 1836

JOHN CLARE

John Clare (1793-1864) was a largely self-educated farm labourer who is now regarded as one of Britain's foremost poets of the countryside.

With arms and legs at work and gentle stroke
That urges switching tail nor mends his pace,
On an old ribbed and weather beaten horse,
The farmer goes jogtrotting to the fair.
Both keep their pace that nothing can provoke
Followed by brindled dog that snuffs the ground
With urging bark and hurries at his heels.
His hat slouched down, and great coat buttoned close
Bellied like hooped keg, and chuffy face
Red as the morning sun, he takes his round
And talks of stock: and when his jobs are done
And Dobbin's hay is eaten from the rack,
He drinks success to corn in language hoarse,
And claps old Dobbin's hide, and potters back.

(From *John Clare Poems Chiefly from Manuscript*; Cobden-Sanderson, London, 1920)

The Advanced Backpacker, 2000

CHRIS TOWNSEND

The modern world is fast, complex, competitive, and always concerned with what happens next. There is always more to do than there is time. The landscape and even the light are mostly artificial. This can be exciting, but all too often it is frustrating, stressful, and exhausting.

In contrast, hiking for weeks or months at a time in an unspoiled natural environment is a simple, repetitive activity that leads to calmness and psychological well-being, a feeling of wholeness, of being a complete person. Each day follows the same pattern, linking in with natural rhythms–walk in the light, sleep in the dark, eat when hungry, take shelter from storms.

... one study found that in regular walkers the hippocampus, an area of the brain essential for memory, actually expanded. Regular walkers have brains that in MRI scans look,

Only the details are different. I get a great pleasure from this simplicity, from the basic pattern of walk and camp, walk and camp. It is good to escape the rush of the modern world and for a period of time to live a quieter, more basic life. Problems and worries subside as the days go by; they are put into perspective by the elemental activity of putting one foot in front of the other hour after hour, day after day.

And on returning from the wilds, restored and revitalized by the experience, I find civilization can be much easier to deal with; indeed, aspects of it can seem very desirable.

(From *The Advanced Backpacker: A Handbook of Year-Round Long-Distance Hiking*; Ragged Mountain Press, McGraw Hill, Camden, 2000, © Chris Townsend)

Walkers Not Welcome, 1782
KARL MORITZ

Moritz was a pastor from Prussia who visited England in 1782, travelling on foot for part of his trip. He travelled light with not much more than his walking cane and a copy of Milton's Paradise Lost. *He much admired the freer form of citizenship exhibited in England, so different from much of Europe at the time. And he was particularly impressed by the beauty of the landscape through which he walked. However, the welcome he received as a walker was decidedly cool.*

A traveller on foot in this country seems to be considered as a sort of wild man or out-of-the-way being, who is stared at, pitied, suspected, and shunned by everybody that meets him. At least this has hitherto been my case on the road from Richmond to Windsor.

My host at Richmond, yesterday morning, could not sufficiently express his surprise that I intended to venture to walk as far as Oxford, and still farther. He however was so kind as to send his son, a clever little boy, to show me the road leading to Windsor.

☆　☆　☆

When I was on the other side of the water, I came to a house and asked a man who was standing at the door if I was on the right road to Oxford. 'Yes', said he, 'but you want a carriage to carry you thither'. When I answered him that I intended walking it, he looked at me significantly, shook his head, and went into the house again.

I was now on the road to Oxford. It is a charming fine broad road, and I met on it carriages without number, which, however, on account of the heat, occasioned a dust that was extremely troublesome and disagreeable. The fine green hedges, which border the roads in England, contribute greatly to render them pleasant. This was the case in the road I now travelled, for when I was tired I sat down in the shade under one of these hedges and read Milton. But this relief was soon rendered disagreeable to me, for those who rode or drove past me, stared at me with astonishment, and made many significant gestures as if they thought my head deranged; so singular must it needs have appeared to them to see a man sitting along the side of a public road and reading. I therefore found myself obliged, when I wished to rest myself and read, to look out for a retired spot in some by-lane or crossroad.

When I again walked, many of the coachmen who drove by called out to me, ever and anon, and asked if I would not ride on the outside; and when, every now and then, a farmer on horseback met me, he said, and seemingly with an air of pity for me, 'Tis warm walking, sir;' and when I passed through a village, every old woman testified her pity by an exclamation of – 'Good God!'

☆   ☆   ☆

The short English miles are delightful for walking. You are always pleased to find, every now and then, in how short a time you have walked a mile, though, no doubt, a mile is everywhere a mile, I walk but a moderate pace, and can accomplish four English miles in an hour. It used to take me pretty nearly the same time for one German mile*. Now it is a pleasing exchange to find that in two hours I can walk eight miles. And now I fancy I was about seventeen miles from London, when I came to an inn, where, for a little wine and water, I was obliged to pay sixpence. An Englishman who happened to be sitting by the side of the

* One *Preußische Landmeile* or 24,000 Prussian ft = 4⅔ Imperial miles or 7.5km

---

Walking is the best possible exercise. Habituate yourself to walk very fast. THOMAS JEFFERSON

innkeeper found out that I was a German, and, of course, from the country of his queen, in praise of whom he was quite lavish, observing more than once that England never had had such a queen, and would not easily get such another.

It now began to grow hot. On the left hand, almost close to the high road, I met with a singularly clear rivulet. In this I bathed, and was much refreshed, and afterwards, with fresh alacrity, continued my journey.

I had now got over the common, and was once more in a country rich and well cultivated beyond all conception. This continued to be the case as far as Slough, which is twenty miles and a half from London, on the way to Oxford, and from which to the left there is a road leading to Windsor, whose high white castle I have already seen at a distance.

I made no stay here, but went directly to the right, along a very pleasant high road, between meadows and green hedges, towards Windsor, where I arrived about noon.

It strikes a foreigner as something particular and unusual when, on passing through these fine English towns, he observed one of those circumstances by which the towns in Germany are distinguished from the villages – no walls, no gates, no sentries, nor garrisons. No stern examiner comes here to search and inspect us or our baggage; no imperious guard here demands a sight of our passports; perfectly free and unmolested, we here walk through villages and towns as unconcerned as we should through a house of our own.

Just before I got to Windsor I passed Eton College, one of the first public schools in England, and perhaps in the world. I have before observed that there are in England fewer of these great schools than one might expect. It lay on my left; and on the right, directly opposite to it, was an inn, into which I went.

☆ ☆ ☆

As I entered the inn, and desired to have something to eat, the countenance of the waiter soon gave me to understand that I should there find no very friendly reception. Whatever I got they seemed to give me with such an air as showed too plainly how little they thought of me, and as if they considered me but as a

Before supper take a little walk; after supper do the same.
ERASMUS

beggar. I must do them the justice to own, however, that they suffered me to pay like a gentleman. No doubt this was the first time this pert, bepowdered puppy had ever been called on to wait on a poor devil who entered their place on foot. I was tired, and asked for a bedroom where I might sleep. They showed me into one that much resembled a prison for malefactors. I requested that I might have a better room at night; on which, without any apology, they told me that they had no intention of lodging me, as they had no room for such guests, but that I might go back to Slough, where very probably I might get a night's lodging.

With money in my pocket, and a consciousness, moreover, that I was doing nothing that was either imprudent, unworthy, or really mean, I own it mortified and vexed me to find myself obliged to put up with this impudent ill-usage from people who ought to reflect that they are but the servants of the public, and little likely to recommend themselves to the high by being insolent to the low. They made me, however, pay them two shillings for my dinner and coffee, which I had just thrown down, and was preparing to shake off the dust from my shoes, and quit this inhospitable St. Christopher, when the green hills of Windsor smiled so friendly upon me, that they seemed to invite me first to visit them.

And now trudging through the streets of Windsor, I at length mounted a sort of hill; a steep path led me on to its summit, close to the walls of the castle, where I had an uncommonly extensive and fine prospect, which so much raised my heart, that in a moment I forgot not only the insults of waiters and tavern-keepers, but the hardship of my lot in being obliged to travel in a manner that exposed me to the scorn of a people whom I wished to respect. Below me lay the most beautiful landscapes in the world – all the rich scenery that nature, in her best attire, can exhibit. Here were the spots that furnished those delightful themes of which the muse of Denham and Pope made choice. I seemed to view a whole world at once, rich and beautiful beyond conception. At that moment what more could I have wished for?

(From *Travels, chiefly on foot, through several parts of England in 1782, described in Letters to a Friend*, trans 1795)

Just watch me walking in all the squares.
A.A. MILNE, *WHEN WE WERE VERY YOUNG*

The Road Not Taken, 1915
ROBERT FROST

It is interesting to compare this poem by Robert Frost (1874-1963) with the less optimistic one written by his friend Edward Thomas (see p43).

Two roads diverged in a yellow wood,
And sorry I could not travel both
And be one traveller, long I stood
And looked down one as far as I could
To where it bent in the undergrowth;

Then took the other, as just as fair,
And having perhaps the better claim,
Because it was grassy and wanted wear;
Though as for that the passing there
Had worn them really about the same,

And both that morning equally lay
In leaves no step had trodden black.
Oh, I kept the first for another day!
Yet knowing how way leads on to way,
I doubted if I should ever come back.

I shall be telling this with a sigh
Somewhere ages and ages hence:
Two roads diverged in a wood, and I –
I took the one less travelled by,
And that has made all the difference.

(From *Mountain Interval*; Henry Holt, New York, 1916, © Robert Frost)

The Passionate Man's Pilgrimage, 1603
SIR WALTER RALEIGH

As well as being an explorer of the New World and the man said to have introduced potatoes and tobacco to Elizabethan England, Raleigh was also an accomplished poet. This poem is said to have been composed by Raleigh in prison the night before he was to be beheaded for treason. On

The best remedy for a short temper is a long walk.
JOSEPH JOUBERT

that occasion, however, he was reprieved.

Give me my scallop-shell of quiet,
My staff of faith to walk upon,
My scrip of joy, immortal diet,
My bottle of salvation,
My gown of glory, hope's true gage;
And thus I'll take my pilgrimage.
Blood must be my body's balmer;
No other balm will there be given:
Whilst my soul, like quiet palmer,
Travelleth towards the land of heaven;
Over the silver mountains,
Where spring the nectar fountains;
There will I kiss
The bowl of bliss;
And drink mine everlasting fill
Upon every milken hill.
My soul will be a-dry before;
But, after, it will thirst no more.

Then by that happy blissful day,
More peaceful pilgrims I shall see,
That have cast off their rags of clay,
And walk apparelled fresh like me.
I'll take them first
To quench their thirst
And taste of nectar suckets,
At those clear wells
Where sweetness dwells,
Drawn up by saints in crystal buckets.

And when our bottles and all we
Are filled with immortality,
Then the blessed paths we'll travel,
Strowed with rubies thick as gravel;
Ceilings of diamonds, sapphire floors,
High walls of coral and pearly bowers.
From thence to heaven's bribeless hall,

After a day's walk everything has twice its usual value. G.M. TREVELYAN

Where no corrupted voices brawl;
No conscience molten into gold,
No forged accuser bought or sold,
No cause deferred, no vain-spent journey,
For there Christ is the king's Attorney,
Who pleads for all without degrees,
And He hath angels, but no fees.
And when the grand twelve-million jury
Of our sins, with direful fury,
Against our souls black verdicts give,
Christ pleads His death, and then we live.

Be Thou my speaker, taintless pleader,
Unblotted lawyer, true proceeder!
Thou givest salvation even for alms;
Not with a bribed lawyer's palms.
And this is mine eternal plea
To Him that made heaven, earth, and sea,
That, since my flesh must die so soon,
And want a head to dine next noon,
Just at the stroke, when my veins start and spread,
Set on my soul an everlasting head!
Then am I ready, like a palmer fit,
To tread those blest paths which before I writ.

(From *Sir Walter Raleigh (1554–1618) Poems*, 1892)

Walking for Mr Darcy, 1813

JANE AUSTEN

Miss Bingley made no answer, and soon afterwards she got up and walked about the room. Her figure was elegant, and she walked well; but Darcy, at whom it was all aimed, was still inflexibly studious. In the desperation of her feelings, she resolved on one effort more, and, turning to Elizabeth, said:

'Miss Eliza Bennet, let me persuade you to follow my example, and take a turn about the room. I assure you it is very refreshing after sitting so long in one attitude.'

Happy is the man who has acquired the love of walking for its own sake. W.J. HOLLAND

GREAT BRITAIN

Elizabeth was surprised, but agreed to it immediately. Miss Bingley succeeded no less in the real object of her civility; Mr. Darcy looked up. He was as much awake to the novelty of attention in that quarter as Elizabeth herself could be, and unconsciously closed his book. He was directly invited to join their party, but he declined it, observing that he could imagine but two motives for their choosing to walk up and down the room together, with either of which motives his joining them would interfere. 'What could he mean? She was dying to know what could be his meaning?' – and asked Elizabeth whether she could at all understand him?

'Not at all,' was her answer; 'but depend upon it, he means to be severe on us, and our surest way of disappointing him will be to ask nothing about it.'

Miss Bingley, however, was incapable of disappointing Mr. Darcy in anything, and persevered therefore in requiring an explanation of his two motives.

'I have not the smallest objection to explaining them,' said he, as soon as she allowed him to speak. 'You either choose this method of passing the evening because you are in each other's confidence, and have secret affairs to discuss, or because you are conscious that your figures appear to the greatest advantage in walking; if the first, I would be completely in your way, and if the second, I can admire you much better as I sit by the fire.'

'Oh! shocking!' cried Miss Bingley. 'I never heard anything so abominable. How shall we punish him for such a speech?'

(From *Pride and Prejudice*; T. Egerton, London, 1813)

Escape from the Asylum, 1841

JOHN CLARE

John Clare (1793-1864) is one of the foremost poets of rural English life. Known as the Northamptonshire Peasant Poet, he was largely self-educated. He had early successes with his published poems but soon found himself torn between his literary life in London and his more humble roots with his family in Northamptonshire. He took to drink and his

---

Adopt the pace of nature: her secret is patience.
RALPH WALDO EMERSON

mental health began to suffer; he believed he was Byron and that had two wives: Mary and Patty. Eventually he had himself admitted to Dr Allen's asylum at Fair Mead House in Essex but soon decides to leave. He documents his 80-mile walk home in his 'Journal'...

'**July 18, 1841, Sunday**. – Felt very melancholy. Went for a walk in the forest in the afternoon. Fell in with some gypsies, one of whom offered to assist in my escape from the madhouse by hiding me in his camp, to which I almost agreed. But I told him I had no money to start with; but if he would do so, I would promise him fifty pounds, and he agreed to do so before Saturday...

July 19, Monday. – Did nothing.

July 20, Tuesday. – Reconnoitred the road the gypsey had taken, and found it a legible (!) one to make a movement; and having only honest courage and myself in my army, I led the way and my troops soon followed. But being careless in mapping down the road as the gypsey told me, I missed the lane to Enfield Town, and was going down Enfield Highway, till I passed the 'Labour-in-vain' public-house, where a person who came out of the door told me the way. I walked down the lane gently, and was soon in Enfield Town, and by and by on the great York Road, where it was all plain sailing. Steering ahead, meeting no enemy and fearing none, I reached Stevenage, where, being night, I got over a gate, and crossed the corner of a green paddock. Seeing a pond or hollow in the corner, I was forced to stay off a respectable distance to keep from falling into it. My legs were nearly knocked up and began to stagger. I scaled over some old rotten palings into the yard, and then had higher palings to clamber over, to get into the shed or hovel; which I did with difficulty, being rather weak. To my good luck, I found some trusses of clover piled up, about six or more feet square, which I gladly mounted and slept on. There were some rags in the hovel, on which I could have reposed had I not found a better bed. I slept soundly, but had a very uneasy dream. I thought my first wife lay on my left arm, and somebody took her away from my side, which made me wake up rather unhappy. I thought as I awoke somebody said 'Mary', but nobody was near. I lay down with my head towards

Make your feet your friend.
J.M. Barrie

the north, to show myself the steering point in the morning.

July 21. – Daylight was looking in on every side, and fearing my garrison might be taken by storm, and myself be made prisoner, I left my lodging by the way I got in, and thanked God for His kindness in procuring it. For anything in a famine is better than nothing, and any place that giveth the weary rest is a blessing. I gained the North Road again, and steered due north. On the left hand side, the road under the bank was like a cave; I saw a man and boy coiled up asleep, whom I hailed, and they awoke to tell me the name of the next village. Somewhere on the London side, near the 'Plough' public-house, a man passed me on horseback, in a slop frock, and said, 'Here's another of the broken-down hay-makers,' and threw me a penny to get a half pint of beer, which I picked up, and thanked him for, and when I got to the 'Plough,' I called for a half pint and drank it. I got a rest, and escaped a very heavy shower in the bargain, by having a shelter till it was over. Afterwards I would have begged a penny off two drovers, but they were very saucy; so I begged no more of anybody.

☆   ☆   ☆

The road was very lonely and dark, being overshaded with trees. At length I came to a place where the road branched off into two turnpikes, one to the right about, and the other straight forward. On going by, I saw a milestone standing under the hedge, and I turned back to read it, to see where the other road led to. I found it led to London. I then suddenly forgot which was north or south, and though I narrowly examined both ways, I could see no tree, or bush, or stone heap that I could recollect having passed.

I went on mile after mile, almost convinced I was going the same way I had come. These thoughts were so strong upon me, and doubts and hopelessness made me turn so feeble, that I was scarcely able to walk. Yet I could not sit down or give up, but shuffled along till I saw a lamp shining as bright as the moon, which, on nearing, I found was suspended over a tollgate. Before I got through, the man came out with a candle, and eyed me narrowly; but having no fear I stopped to ask him whether I was

A vigorous five-mile walk will do more good for an unhappy but otherwise healthy adult than all the medicine and psychology in the world. Paul Dudley White

going northward. He said, 'When you get through the gate you are.' I thanked him, and went through to the other side, and gathered my old strength as my doubts vanished. I soon cheered up, and hummed the air of 'Highland Mary' as I went on. I at length came to an odd house, all alone, near a wood; but I could not see what the sign was, though it seemed to stand, oddly enough, in a sort of trough, or spout. There was a large porch over the door, and being weary I crept in, and was glad enough to find I could lie with my legs straight. The inmates were all gone to rest, for I could hear them turn over in bed, while I lay at full length on the stones in the porch. I slept here till daylight, and felt very much refreshed. I blest my two wives and both their families when I laid down and when I got up in the morning.

☆   ☆   ☆

The third day I satisfied my hunger by eating the grass on the roadside, which seemed to taste something like bread. I was hungry, and ate heartily till I was satisfied; in fact, the meal seemed to do me good. The next and last day I remembered that I had some tobacco, and my box of lucifers being exhausted, I could not light my pipe. So I took to chewing tobacco all day, and ate it when I had done. I was never hungry afterwards. I remember passing through Buckden, and going a length of road afterwards; but I do not recollect the name of any place until I came to Stilton, where I was completely footsore, bleeding, and broken down. When I had got about half way through the town, a gravel causeway invited me to rest myself; so I laid down and nearly went to sleep. A young woman, as I guessed by the voice, came out of a house, and said, 'Poor creature;' and another more elderly said, 'Oh, he shams.' But when I got up the latter said, 'Oh no, he don't,' as I hobbled along very lame. I heard the voices, but never looked back to see where they came from. When I got near the inn at the end of the gravel walk, I met two young women, and asked one of them whether the road branching to the right by the inn did not lead to Peterborough. She said, 'Yes.' As soon as ever I was on it, I felt myself on the way home, and went on rather more cheerful, though I was forced to rest oftener than usual.

Before I got to Peterborough, a man and woman passed in a

The English winter – ending in July to recommence in August. BYRON, *DON JUAN*

cart; and on hailing me as they passed, I found they were neighbours from Helpston, where I used to live. I told them I was
knocked-up, which they could easily see, and that I had neither
food nor drink since I left Essex. When I had told my story they
clubbed together and threw me fivepence out of the cart. I picked
it up, and called at a small public-house near the bridge, where I
had two half pints of ale, and twopennyworth of bread and
cheese. When I had done, I started quite refreshed; only my feet
were more crippled than ever, and I could scarcely bear walk
over the stones. Yet I was half ashamed to sit down in the street,
and forced myself to keep on the move.

I got through Peterborough better than I expected. When I
came to the high road, I rested on the stone-heaps, till I was able
to go on afresh. By-and-by I passed Walton, and soon reached
Werrington. I was making for the 'Beehive' as fast as I could when
a cart met me, with a man, a woman, and a boy in it. When nearing me the woman jumped out and caught fast hold of my hands,
and wished me to get into the cart. But I refused; I thought her
either drunk or mad. But when I was told it was my second wife,
Patty, I got in, and was soon at Northborough. But Mary was not
there; neither could I get any information about her further than
the old story of her having died six years ago. But I took no notice
of the lie, having seen her myself twelve months ago, alive and
well, and as young as ever. So here I am hopeless at home.'

(From *The Life of John Clare* by Frederick Martin, Macmillan & Co, London, 1865)

The Winter's Spring, 1841

JOHN CLARE

On a winter walk the poet celebrates the coldest time of year.

> The winter comes; I walk alone,
> I want no bird to sing;
> To those who keep their hearts their own
> The winter is the spring.
> No flowers to please–no bees to hum–
> The coming spring's already come.

**Walking and talking are two very great pleasures, but it is a
mistake to combine them. Our own noise blots out the
sounds and silences of the outdoor world; and talking**

I never want the Christmas rose
To come before its time;
The seasons, each as God bestows,
Are simple and sublime.
I love to see the snowstorm hing;
'Tis but the winter garb of spring.
I never want the grass to bloom:
The snowstorm's best in white.
I love to see the tempest come
And love its piercing light.
The dazzled eyes that love to cling
O'er snow-white meadows see the spring.
I love the snow, the crumpling snow
That hangs on everything,
It covers everything below
Like white dove's brooding wing,
A landscape to the aching sight,
A vast expanse of dazzling light.
It is the foliage of the woods
That winters bring–the dress,
White Easter of the year in bud,
That makes the winter Spring.
The frost and snow his posies bring,
Nature's white spurts of the spring.

(From *John Clare Poems Chiefly from Manuscript*; Cobden-Sanderson, London, 1920)

The Go-Between, 1900

L.P. HARTLEY

Twelve-year-old Leo, staying with his aristocratic friend Marcus and his family in Norfolk, becomes a secret go-between taking messages for Marcus's sister Marian and her lover, the local farmer Ted Burgess.

Between the next day, Tuesday, and the cricket match, which was on Saturday, I three times carried messages between Marian and Ted Burgess: three notes from her, one note and two verbal messages from him.

leads almost inevitably to smoking, and then farewell to nature as far as one of our senses is concerned.

C.S. LEWIS

'Tell her it's all right,' he said the first time; then: 'Tell her it's no go.'

It wasn't difficult to find him, for he was usually working in the harvest fields on the far side of the river; from the sluice platform I could see where he was. The first time I went he was riding on the reaper, a new-fangled machine which cut the corn, but did not bind it; it was called the 'Spring-balance', I remember. I walked beside it until the standing corn was between us and the three or four farm-labourers who were binding the sheaves, and then he stopped the horse and I handed him the letter.

Next day the area of uncut corn had dwindled; and he was standing with his gun watching for the rabbits and other creatures which clung to their shelter till the last moment before bolting out; this was so exciting that for a time I quite forgot the letter and he stood with narrowed eyes apparently having forgotten it too.

My excitement mounted for I thought that this last stronghold would be stuffed with game; but I was wrong: the last stalks fell and nothing came out.

The man on the reaper drove it off towards the gate that led to the next field; turning their backs on us the labourers plodded to the hedgerow to retrieve their coats and rush-baskets. The farmer and I were left alone.

The field that had been cut looked very flat, and he was much the tallest thing in it. Standing there, the colour of the corn, between red and gold, I had the fancy that he was a sheaf the reaper had forgotten and that it would come back for him.

I gave him the envelope which he at once tore open; and then I knew that he must have killed something before I came, for, to my horror, a long smear of blood appeared on the envelope and again on the letter as he held it in his hands.

I cried out: 'Oh, don't do that!' but he did not answer me, he was so engrossed in reading.

The other time I went in search of him he was not in the field but in the farmyard and it was then he gave me the letter to take back.

'No blood on this one,' he said humorously, and I laughed,

A journey is best measured in friends, rather than miles. TIM CAHILL

for there was a part of me that accepted the blood and even rejoiced in it as part of a man's life into which I should one day be initiated. I had a great time sliding down the straw-stack; indeed I did this on all three occasions when I took him letters; it was the climax of the expedition and when I got back to the party reassembled at tea, I was able to tell them with perfect truth that that was how I spent my afternoons.

(From *The Go-Between*; Hamish Hamilton, 1953, © LP Hartley)

Climbing Ben Lomond, 1846

BAYARD TAYLOR

Taylor's first trip abroad was to Europe in 1846, when he was 21. He had been apprenticed to a printer in West Chester, Pennsylvania in 1842 and had had some success publishing poetry he had written. He set off on his 19th century gap year to see the sights of Europe on foot, taking a Liverpool packet from New York for a journey which owing to bad weather took almost a month. Two further trips by boat bring him to Loch Lomond...

When we arose in the morning, at 4 o'clock, to return with the boat, the sun was already shining upon the westward hills, scarcely a cloud was in the sky, and the air was pure and cool. To our great delight Ben Lomond was unshrouded, and we were told that a more favorable day for the ascent had not occurred for two months. We left the boat at Rowardennan, an inn at the southern base of Ben Lomond. After breakfasting on Loch Lomond trout, I stole out to the shore while my companions were preparing for the ascent, and made a hasty sketch of the lake.

We purposed descending on the northern side and crossing the Highlands to Loch Katrine; though it was represented as difficult and dangerous by the guide who wished to accompany us, we determined to run the risk of being enveloped in a cloud on the summit, and so set out alone, the path appearing plain before us. We had no difficulty in following it up the lesser heights, around the base. It wound on, over rock and bog, among the heather and broom with which the mountain is covered, some-

If your dog is fat, you're not getting enough exercise.
ANON

times running up a steep acclivity, and then winding zigzag round a rocky ascent. The rains two days before, had made the bogs damp and muddy, but with this exception, we had little trouble for some time. Ben Lomond is a doubly formed mountain. For about three-fourths of the way there is a continued ascent, when it is suddenly terminated by a large barren plain, from one end of which the summit shoots up abruptly, forming at the north side, a precipice 500 feet high. As we approached the summit of the first part of the mountain, the way became very steep and toilsome; but the prospect, which had before been only on the south side, began to open on the east, and we saw suddenly spread out below us, the vale of Menteith, with 'far Loch Ard and Aberfoil' in the centre, and the huge front of Benvenue filling up the picture. Taking courage from this, we hurried on. The heather had become stunted and dwarfish, and the ground was covered with short brown grass. The mountain sheep, which we saw looking at us from the rock above, had worn so many paths along the side, that we could not tell which to take, but pushed on in the direction of the summit, till thinking it must be near at hand, we found a mile and a half of plain before us, with the top of Ben Lomond at the farther end. The plain was full of wet moss, crossed in all directions by deep ravines or gullies worn in it by the mountain rains, and the wind swept across with a tempest-like force.

I met, near the base, a young gentleman from Edinburgh, who had left Rowardennan before us, and we commenced ascending together. It was hard work, but neither liked to stop, so we climbed up to the first resting place, and found the path leading along the brink of a precipice. We soon attained the summit, and climbing up a little mound of earth and stones, I saw the half of Scotland at a glance. The clouds hung just above the mountain tops, which rose all around like the waves of a mighty sea. On every side – near and far – stood their misty summits, but Ben Lomond was the monarch of them all. Loch Lomond lay unrolled under my feet like a beautiful map, and just opposite, Loch Long thrust its head from between the feet of the crowded hills, to catch a glimpse of the giant. We could see from Ben Nevis to

Away, away, from men and towns,
To the wild wood and the downs,
To the silent wilderness,

Ayr – from Edinburgh to Staffa. Stirling and Edinburgh Castles would have been visible, but that the clouds hung low in the valley of the Forth and hid them from our sight.

The view from Ben Lomond is nearly twice as extensive as that from Catskill, being uninterrupted on every side, but it wants the glorious forest scenery, clear, blue sky, and active, rejoicing character of the latter. We stayed about two hours upon the summit, taking refuge behind the cairn, when the wind blew strong. I found the smallest of flowers under a rock, and brought it away as a memento. In the middle of the precipice there is a narrow ravine or rather cleft in the rock, to the bottom, from whence the mountain slopes regularly but steeply down to the valley. At the bottom we stopped to awake the echoes, which were repeated four times; our German companion sang the Hunter's Chorus, which resounded magnificently through this Highland hall. We drank from the river Forth, which starts from a spring at the foot of the rock, and then commenced descending. This was also toilsome enough. The mountain was quite wet and covered with loose stones, which, dislodged by our feet, went rattling down the side, oftentimes to the danger of the foremost ones; and when we had run or rather slid down the three miles, to the bottom, our knees trembled so as scarcely to support us.

(From *Views A-Foot; Europe Seen with Knapsack and Staff*; Wiley & Putnam, New York, 1846)

Setting Out, 1934

LAURIE LEE

Laurie Lee (1914-97) sets out for Spain, leaving his home in the Gloucestershire village of Slad on the journey recounted in As I Walked Out One Midsummer Morning, *the second volume of the trilogy which began with* Cider With Rosie *and ended with* A Moment of War.

The stooping figure of my mother, waist-deep in the grass and caught there like a piece of sheep's wool, was the last I saw of my country home as I left it to discover the world. She stood old and

**Where the soul need not repress
Its music.**
PERCY BYSSHE SHELLEY

bent at the top of the bank, silently watching me go, one gnarled red hand raised in farewell and blessing, not questioning why I went. At the bend of the road I looked back again and saw the gold light die behind her; then I turned the corner, passed the village school, and closed that part of my life for ever.

It was a bright Sunday morning in early June, the right time to be leaving home. My three sisters and a brother had already gone before me; two other brothers had yet to make up their minds. They were still sleeping that morning, but my mother had got up early and cooked me a heavy breakfast, had stood wordlessly while I ate it, her hand on my chair, and had then helped me pack up my few belongings. There had been no fuss, no appeals, no attempts at advice or persuasion, only a long and searching look. Then, with my bags on my back, I'd gone out into the early sunshine and climbed through the long wet grass to the road.

It was 1934. I was nineteen years old, still soft at the edges, but with a confident belief in good fortune. I carried a small rolled-up tent, a violin in a blanket, a change of clothes, a tin of treacle biscuits, and some cheese. I was excited, vainglorious, knowing I had far to go; but not, as yet, how far. As I left home that morning and walked away from the sleeping village, it never occurred to me that others had done this before me.

I was propelled, of course, by the traditional forces that had sent many generations along this road – by the small tight valley closing in around one, stifling the breath with its mossy mouth, the cottage walls narrowing like the arms of an iron maiden, the local girls whispering, 'Marry, and settle down.' Months of restless unease, leading to this inevitable moment, had been spent wandering about the hills, mournfully whistling, and watching the high open fields stepping away eastwards under gigantic clouds ...

And now I was on my journey, in a pair of thick boots and with a hazel stick in my hand. Naturally, I was going to London, which lay a hundred miles to the east; and it seemed equally obvious that I should go on foot. But first, as I'd never yet seen the sea, I thought I'd walk to the coast and find it. This would add another hundred miles to my journey, going by way of

Walking is good for solving problems – it's like the feet are little psychiatrists. TERRI GUILLEMETS

Southampton. But I had all the summer and all time to spend.

That first day alone – and now I was really alone at last – steadily declined in excitement and vigour. As I tramped through the dust towards the Wiltshire Downs a growing reluctance weighed me down. White elder-blossom and dog-roses hung in the hedges, blank as unwritten paper, and the hot empty road – there were few motor cars then – reflected Sunday's waste and indifference. High sulky summer sucked me towards it, and I offered no resistance at all. Through the solitary morning and afternoon I found myself longing for some opposition or rescue, for the sound of hurrying footsteps coming after me and family voices calling me back. None came. I was free. I was affronted by freedom. The day's silence said, Go where you will, It's all yours. You asked for it. It's up to you now, You're on your own, and nobody's going to stop you.

(From *As I Walked Out One Midsummer Morning*; André Deutsch, London; Atheneum, New York: 1969, © Laurie Lee)

The Sign-Post, 1916

EDWARD THOMAS

Edward Thomas (1878-1917) and Robert Frost were friends who used to walk together so it is not surprising that there are similar themes in this poem and Frost's The Road Not Taken *(see p29). Thomas did not begin to write poetry until the last three years of his life and died in 1917 at the Battle of Arras. He is buried in France.*

The dim sea glints chill. The white sun is shy,
And the skeleton weeds and the never-dry,
Rough, long grasses keep white with frost
At the hilltop by the finger-post;
The smoke of the traveller's-joy is puffed
Over hawthorn berry and hazel tuft.
I read the sign. Which way shall I go?
A voice says: You would not have doubted so
At twenty. Another voice gentle with scorn
Says: At twenty you wished you had never been born.

The human spirit needs places where nature has not been rearranged by the hand of man. ANON

One hazel lost a leaf of gold
From a tuft at the tip, when the first voice told
The other he wished to know what 'twould be
To be sixty by this same post. 'You shall see,'
He laughed – and I had to join his laughter –
'You shall see; but either before or after,
Whatever happens, it must befall,
A mouthful of earth to remedy all
Regrets and wishes shall freely be given;
And if there be a flaw in that heaven
'Twill be freedom to wish, and your wish may be
To be here or anywhere talking to me,
No matter what the weather, on earth,
At any age between death and birth,
To see what day or night can be,
The sun and the frost, the land and the sea,
Summer, Autumn, Winter, Spring, –
With a poor man of any sort, down to a king,
Standing upright out in the air
Wondering where he shall journey, O where?'

(From *Poems*; Selwyn & Blount, London, 1917)

The Proposal, 1867

ANTHONY TROLLOPE

In this novel that follows the political career and love life of the hand-some Phineas Finn, Anthony Trollope (1815-82) explores British par-liamentary politics and society of the 1860s. Phineas Finn has won a seat in parliament and decides to ask Lady Laura Standish, daughter of the wealthy politician Lord Brentford, for her hand in marriage.

They went up the path by the brook, from bridge to bridge, till they found themselves out upon the open mountain at the top. Phineas had resolved that he would not speak out his mind till he found himself on that spot; that then he would ask her to sit down, and that while she was so seated he would tell her every-thing. At the present moment he had on his head a Scotch cap

There is nothing like walking to get the feel of a country. A fine landscape is like a piece of music; it must be taken at with a grouse's feather in it, and he was dressed in a velvet shoot-ing-jacket and dark knickerbockers; and was certainly, in this cos-tume, as handsome a man as any woman would wish to see. And there was, too, a look of breeding about him which had come to him, no doubt, from the royal Finns of old, which ever served him in great stead. He was, indeed, only Phineas Finn, and was known by the world to be no more; but he looked as though he might have been anybody, – a royal Finn himself. And then he had that special grace of appearing to be altogether unconscious of his own personal advantages. And I think that in truth he was barely conscious of them; that he depended on them very little, if at all; that there was nothing of personal vanity in his composi-tion. He had never indulged in any hope that Lady Laura would accept him because he was a handsome man.

'After all that climbing,' he said, 'will you not sit down for a moment?' As he spoke to her she looked at him and told herself that he was as handsome as a god. 'Do sit down for one moment,' he said. 'I have something that I desire to say to you, and to say it here.'

'I will,' she said; 'but I also have something to tell you, and will say it while I am yet standing. Yesterday I accepted an offer of marriage from Mr. Kennedy.'

'Then I am too late,' said Phineas, and putting his hands into the pockets of his coat, he turned his back upon her, and walked away across the mountain.

What a fool he had been to let her know his secret when her knowledge of it could be of no service to him, – when her knowl-edge of it could only make him appear foolish in her eyes! But for his life he could not have kept his secret to himself. Nor now could he bring himself to utter a word of even decent civility. But he went on walking as though he could thus leave her there, and never see her again. What an ass he had been in supposing that she cared for him! What a fool to imagine that his poverty could stand a chance against the wealth of Loughlinter! But why had she lured him on? How he wished that he were now grinding, hard at work in Mr. Low's chambers, or sitting at home at Killaloe with the hand of that pretty little Irish girl within his own!

the right tempo. Even a bicycle goes too fast.
PAUL SCOTT MOWRER, *THE HOUSE OF EUROPE*

Presently he heard a voice behind him, – calling him gently. Then he turned and found that she was very near him. He himself had then been standing still for some moments, and she had followed him. 'Mr. Finn,' she said.

'Well; – yes: what is it?' And turning round he made an attempt to smile.

'Will you not wish me joy, or say a word of congratulation? Had I not thought much of your friendship, I should not have been so quick to tell you of my destiny. No one else has been told, except papa.'

'Of course I hope you will be happy. Of course I do. No wonder he lent me the pony!'

'You must forget all that.'

'Forget what?'

'Well, – nothing. You need forget nothing,' said Lady Laura, 'for nothing has been said that need be regretted. Only wish me joy, and all will be pleasant.'

'Lady Laura, I do wish you joy, with all my heart, – but that will not make all things pleasant. I came up here to ask you to be my wife.'

'No; – no no; do not say it.'

☆   ☆   ☆

Phineas had now seated himself on the exact stone on which he had wished her to sit when he proposed to tell his own story, and was looking forth upon the lake. It seemed to him that everything had been changed for him while he had been up there upon the mountain, and that the change had been marvellous in its nature. When he had been coming up, there had been apparently two alternatives before him: the glory of successful love, – which, indeed, had seemed to him to be a most improbable result of the coming interview, – and the despair and utter banishment attendant on disdainful rejection. But his position was far removed from either of these alternatives. She had almost told him that she would have loved him had she not been poor, – that she was beginning to love him and had quenched her love, because it had become impossible to her to marry a poor man. In

I want to walk through life instead of being dragged through it. ALANIS MORISSETTE

such circumstances he could not be angry with her, – he could not quarrel with her; he could not do other than swear to himself that he would be her friend. And yet he loved her better than ever; – and she was the promised wife of his rival! Why had not Donald Bean's pony broken his neck?

'Shall we go down now?' she said.

(From *Phineas Finn – The Irish Member*; Virtue & Co, London, 1869)

The Rolling English Road, 1913

G.K. CHESTERTON

When this poem was first published it was entitled A Song of Temperance Reform. *It was written in protest against the possible introduction of prohibition into Britain.*

Before the Roman came to Rye or out to Severn strode,
The rolling English drunkard made the rolling English road.
A reeling road, a rolling road, that rambles round the shire,
And after him the parson ran, the sexton and the squire;
A merry road, a mazy road, and such as we did tread
The night we went to Birmingham by way of Beachy Head.

I knew no harm of Bonaparte and plenty of the Squire,
And for to fight the Frenchman I did not much desire;
But I did bash their baggonets because they came arrayed
To straighten out the crooked road an English drunkard made,
Where you and I went down the lane with ale-mugs in our
        hands,
The night we went to Glastonbury by way of Goodwin Sands.

His sins they were forgiven him; or why do flowers run
Behind him; and the hedges all strengthening in the sun?
The wild thing went from left to right and knew not which
        was which,
But the wild rose was above him when they found him in the
        ditch.
God pardon us, nor harden us; we did not see so clear
The night we went to Bannockburn by way of Brighton Pier.

**In every walk with nature one receives far more
than one seeks.** JOHN MUIR

My friends, we will not go again or ape an ancient rage,
Or stretch the folly of our youth to be the shame of age,
But walk with clearer eyes and ears this path that wandereth,
And see undrugged in evening light the decent inn of death;
For there is good news yet to hear and fine things to be seen,
Before we go to Paradise by way of Kensal Green.

(From *The Collected Poems of G. K. Chesterton*; 1927)

The Roots of Routes and Learning, 2012

ROBERT MACFARLANE

Macfarlane's The Old Ways *is a meditative and poetic investigation of the network of the paths, tracks and ways crossing Britain and beyond and what it is to walk along them.*

The relationship between thinking and walking is also grained deep into language history, illuminated by perhaps the most wonderful etymology I know. The trail begins with our verb *to learn*, meaning 'to acquire knowledge'. Moving backwards in language time, we reach the Old English *leornian*, 'to get knowledge, to be cultivated'. From *leornian* the path leads further back, into the fricative thickets of Proto-Germanic, and to the word *liznojan*, which has a base sense of 'to follow or to find a track' (from the Proto-Indo-European prefix *leis-*, meaning 'track'). 'To learn' therefore means at root – at route – 'to follow a track'. Who knew? Not I, and I am grateful to the etymologist-explorers who uncovered those lost trails connecting 'learning' with 'path-following'.

(From *The Old Ways – A Journey on Foot*; Hamish Hamilton,
London, 2012, © Robert Macfarlane)

The Way, 1969

BRUCE CHATWIN

Gradually the idea for a book began to take shape. It was to be a wildly ambitious and intolerant work, a kind of 'Anatomy of Restlessness' that would enlarge on Pascal's dictum about the

Walking is not simply therapeutic for oneself but it is a

man sitting quietly in a room. The argument, roughly, was as follows: that in becoming human, man had acquired, together with his straight legs and striding walk, a migratory 'drive' or instinct to walk long distances through the seasons; that this 'drive' was inseparable from his central nervous system; and, that, when warped in conditions of settlement, it found outlets in violence, greed, status-seeking or a mania for the new. This would explain why mobile societies such as the gypsies were egalitarian, thing-free and resistant to change; also why, to re-establish the harmony of the First State, all the great teachers – Buddha, Lao-tse, St Francis – had set the perpetual pilgrimage at the heart of their message and told their disciples, literally, to follow The Way.

(From *Anatomy of Restlessness: Selected Writings, 1969-1989*; Jonathan Cape, London, 1997, © Bruce Chatwin)

Club-walking, 1891

THOMAS HARDY

Thomas Hardy (1840-1928) introduces us to the heroine of this novel as she joins local women taking part in a Dorset May Day tradition known as 'club-walking'.

The forests have departed, but some old customs of their shades remain. Many, however, linger only in a metamorphosed or disguised form. The May-Day dance, for instance, was to be discerned on the afternoon under notice, in the guise of the club revel, or 'club-walking,' as it was there called.

It was an interesting event to the younger inhabitants of Marlott, though its real interest was not observed by the participators in the ceremony. Its singularity lay less in the retention of a custom of walking in procession and dancing on each anniversary than in the members being solely women. In men's clubs such celebrations were, though expiring, less uncommon; but either the natural shyness of the softer sex, or a sarcastic attitude on the part of male relatives, had denuded such women's clubs as remained (if any other did) or this their glory and consummation. The club of Marlott alone lived to uphold the local Cerealia. It

poetic activity that can cure the world of all its ills.
BRUCE CHATWIN

had walked for hundreds of years, if not as benefit-club, as votive sisterhood of some sort; and it walked still.

The banded ones were all dressed in white gowns – a gay survival from Old Style days, when cheerfulness and May-time were synonyms – days before the habit of taking long views had reduced emotions to a monotonous average. Their first exhibition of themselves was in a processional march of two and two round the parish. Ideal and real clashed slightly as the sun lit up their figures against the green hedges and creeper-laced house-fronts; for, though the whole troop wore white garments, no two whites were alike among them. Some approached pure blanching; some had a bluish pallor; some worn by the older characters (which had possibly lain by folded for many a year) inclined to a cadaverous tint, and to a Georgian style.

In addition to the distinction of a white frock, every woman and girl carried in her right hand a peeled willow wand, and in her left a bunch of white flowers. The peeling of the former, and the selection of the latter, had been an operation of personal care.

There were a few middle-aged and even elderly women in the train, their silver-wiry hair and wrinkled faces, scourged by time and trouble, having almost a grotesque, certainly a pathetic, appearance in such a jaunty situation. In a true view, perhaps, there was more to be gathered and told of each anxious and experienced one, to whom the years were drawing nigh when she should say, 'I have no pleasure in them,' than of her juvenile comrades. But let the elder be passed over here for those under whose bodices the life throbbed quick and warm.

The young girls formed, indeed, the majority of the band, and their heads of luxuriant hair reflected in the sunshine every tone of gold, and black, and brown. Some had beautiful eyes, others a beautiful nose, others a beautiful mouth and figure: few, if any, had all. A difficulty of arranging their lips in this crude exposure to public scrutiny, an inability to balance their heads, and to dissociate self-consciousness from their features, was apparent in them, and showed that they were genuine country girls, unaccustomed to many eyes.

And as each and all of them were warmed without by the

To climb steep hills requires a slow pace at first.
WILLIAM SHAKESPEARE

sun, so each had a private little sun for her soul to bask in; some dream, some affection, some hobby, at least some remote and distant hope which, though perhaps starving to nothing, still lived on, as hopes will. They were all cheerful, and many of them merry.

They came round by The Pure Drop Inn, and were turning out of the high road to pass through a wicket-gate into the meadows, when one of the women said –

'The Lord-a-Lord! Why, Tess Durbeyfield, if there isn't thy father riding home in a carriage!'

A young member of the band turned her head at the exclamation. She was a fine and handsome girl – not handsomer than some others, possibly – but her mobile peony mouth and large innocent eyes added eloquence to colour and shape. She wore a red ribbon in her hair, and was the only one of the white company who could boast of such a pronounced adornment. As she looked round Durbeyfield was seen moving along the road in a chaise belonging to The Pure Drop, driven by a frizzle-headed brawny damsel with her gown-sleeves rolled above her elbows. This was the cheerful servant of that establishment, who, in her part of factotum, turned groom and ostler at times. Durbeyfield, leaning back, and with his eyes closed luxuriously, was waving his hand above his head, and singing in a slow recitative –

'I've-got-a-gr't-family-vault-at-Kingsbere – and knighted-forefathers-in-lead-coffins-there!'

The clubbists tittered, except the girl called Tess – in whom a slow heat seemed to rise at the sense that her father was making himself foolish in their eyes.

'He's tired, that's all,' she said hastily, 'and he has got a lift home, because our own horse has to rest to-day.'

'Bless thy simplicity, Tess,' said her companions. 'He's got his market-nitch. Haw-haw!'

'Look here; I won't walk another inch with you, if you say any jokes about him!' Tess cried, and the colour upon her cheeks spread over her face and neck. In a moment her eyes grew moist, and her glance drooped to the ground. Perceiving that they had really pained her they said no more, and order again prevailed.

The distance is nothing when one has a motive.
ELIZABETH BENNETT IN *PRIDE AND PREJUDICE*

Tess's pride would not allow her to turn her head again, to learn what her father's meaning was, if he had any; and thus she moved on with the whole body to the enclosure where there was to be dancing on the green. By the time the spot was reached she has recovered her equanimity, and tapped her neighbour with her wand and talked as usual.

Tess Durbeyfield at this time of her life was a mere vessel of emotion untinctured by experience.

(From *Tess of the d'Urbervilles: A Pure Woman*; Macmillan, London, 1891)

The Perfect Walk, 1821

WILLIAM HAZLITT

This excerpt is from an essay entitled On Going a Journey *by William Hazlitt (1778-1830), probably the first piece written specifically on the subject of recreational walking.*

One of the pleasantest things in the world is going a journey; but I like to go by myself. I can enjoy society in a room; but out of doors nature is company enough for me. I am then never less alone than when alone.

'The fields his study, nature was his book.'

I cannot see the wit of walking and talking at the same time. When I am in the country, I wish to vegetate like the country. I am not for criticising hedgerows and black cattle. I go out of town in order to forget the town and all that is in it. There are those who for this purpose go to watering-places, and carry the metropolis with them. I like more elbow-room, and fewer encumbrances. I like solitude, when I give myself up to it, for the sake of solitude ; nor do I ask for

'a friend in my retreat,
Whom I may whisper solitude is sweet.'

The soul of a journey is liberty, perfect liberty, to think, feel, do, just as one pleases. We go a journey chiefly to be free of all impediments and of all inconveniences; to leave ourselves behind, much more to get rid of others. It is because I want a little breathing-space to muse on indifferent matters, where

I can enjoy society in a room; but out of doors, nature is company enough for me.
WILLIAM HAZLITT

Contemplation
> 'May plume her feathers and let grow her wings,
> That in the various bustle of resort
> Were all too ruffled, and sometimes impair'd,'

that I absent myself from the town for a while, without feeling at a loss the moment I am left by myself. Instead of a friend in a post-chaise or in a Tilbury, to exchange good things with and vary the same stale topics over again, for once let me have a truce with impertinence.

Give me the clear blue sky over my head and the green turf beneath my feet, a winding road before me, and a three hours' march to dinner and then to thinking!

(From William Hazlitt, Selections from his Writings;
Frederick Warne & Co, London, 1889)

The Table and the Chair, 1871
EDWARD LEAR

Although Edward Lear (1812-88) was also an accomplished painter and musician, it is for his limericks and other humorous verse that he is chiefly remembered.

I

Said the Table to the Chair,
'You can hardly be aware,
'How I suffer from the heat,
'And from chilblains on my feet!
'If we took a little walk,
'We might have a little talk!
'Pray let us take the air!'
Said the Table to the Chair.

II

Said the Chair unto the Table,
'Now you know we are not able!
'How foolishly you talk,
'When you know we *cannot* walk!'
Said the Table, with a sigh,

... there's music in water. Brooks babbling, fountains splashing. Weirs, waterfalls; tumbling, gushing.
JULIE ANDREWS

'It can do no harm to try,
'I've as many legs as you,
'Why can't we walk on two?'

III

So they both went slowly down,
And walked about the town
With a cheerful bumpy sound,
As they toddled round and round.
And everybody cried,
As they hastened to their side,
'See! the Table and the Chair
'Have come out to take the air!'

IV

But in going down an alley,
To a castle in a valley,
They completely lost their way,
And wandered all the day,
Till, to see them safely back,
They paid a Ducky-quack,
And a Beetle, and a Mouse,
Who took them to their house.

V

Then they whispered to each other,
'O delightful little brother!
'What a lovely walk we've taken!
'Let us dine on Beans and Bacon!'
So the Ducky, and the leetle
Browny-Mousy and the Beetle
Dined, and danced upon their heads
Till they toddled to their beds.

(From *Nonsense Songs, Stories, Botany and Alphabets*; RJ Bush, London, 1871)

I like long walks, especially when they are taken by people who annoy me. NOËL COWARD

The Engagement, 1813

JANE AUSTEN

'Good gracious!' cried Mrs. Bennet, as she stood at a window the next morning, 'if that disagreeable Mr. Darcy is not coming here again with our dear Bingley! What can he mean by being so tiresome as to be always coming here? I had no notion but he would go a-shooting, or something or other, and not disturb us with his company. What shall we do with him? Lizzy, you must walk out with him again, that he may not be in Bingley's way.'

Elizabeth could hardly help laughing at so convenient a proposal; yet was really vexed that her mother should be always giving him such an epithet.

As soon as they entered, Bingley looked at her so expressively, and shook hands with such warmth, as left no doubt of his good information; and he soon afterwards said aloud, 'Mrs. Bennet, have you no more lanes hereabouts in which Lizzy may lose her way again to-day?'

'I advise Mr. Darcy, and Lizzy, and Kitty,' said Mrs. Bennet, 'to walk to Oakham Mount this morning. It is a nice long walk, and Mr. Darcy has never seen the view.'

'It may do very well for the others,' replied Mr. Bingley; 'but I am sure it will be too much for Kitty. Won't it, Kitty?' Kitty owned that she had rather stay at home. Darcy professed a great curiosity to see the view from the Mount, and Elizabeth silently consented. As she went up stairs to get ready, Mrs. Bennet followed her, saying:

'I am quite sorry, Lizzy, that you should be forced to have that disagreeable man all to yourself. But I hope you will not mind it: it is all for Jane's sake, you know; and there is no occasion for talking to him, except just now and then. So, do not put yourself to inconvenience.'

During their walk, it was resolved that Mr. Bennet's consent should be asked in the course of the evening. Elizabeth reserved to herself the application for her mother's. She could not determine how her mother would take it; sometimes doubting whether all his wealth and grandeur would be enough to over-come her abhorrence of the man. But whether she were violently set against the match, or violently delighted with it, it was certain that her manner would be equally ill adapted to do credit to her sense; and she could no more bear that Mr. Darcy should hear the first raptures of her joy, than the first vehemence of her disap-probation.

In the evening, soon after Mr. Bennet withdrew to the library, she saw Mr. Darcy rise also and follow him, and her agitation on seeing it was extreme. She did not fear her father's opposition, but he was going to be made unhappy; and that it should be through her means – that she, his favourite child, should be dis-tressing him by her choice, should be filling him with fears and regrets in disposing of her – was a wretched reflection, and she sat in misery till Mr. Darcy appeared again, when, looking at him, she was a little relieved by his smile. In a few minutes he approached the table where she was sitting with Kitty; and, while pretending to admire her work said in a whisper, 'Go to your father, he wants you in the library.' She was gone directly.

Her father was walking about the room, looking grave and anxious. 'Lizzy,' said he, 'what are you doing? Are you out of your senses, to be accepting this man? Have not you always hated him?'

(From *Pride and Prejudice*; T. Egerton, London, 1813)

After your Walk, 1891
ROBERT LOUIS STEVENSON

Robert Louis Stevenson (1850-94) had read William Hazlitt's essay On Going a Journey *(see p52) and thought it 'so good that there should be a tax levied on all who have not read it'. He went on to write a reply,* Walking Tours, *noting that the benefits of walking continue even after the walk...*

But it is at night, and after dinner, that the best hour comes. There are no such pipes to be smoked as those that follow a good day's march; the flavour of the tobacco is a thing to be remembered, it

If you can walk with Kings – nor lose the common touch ...
RUDYARD KIPLING, *REWARDS AND FAIRIES*

is so dry and aromatic, so full and so fine. If you wind up the evening with grog, you will own there was never such grog; at every sip a jocund tranquillity spreads about your limbs, and sits easily in your heart.

☆   ☆   ☆

If the evening be fine and warm, there is nothing better in life than to lounge before the inn door in the sunset, or lean over the parapet of the bridge, to watch the weeds and the quick fishes. It is then, if ever, that you taste Joviality to the full significance of that audacious word. Your muscles are so agreeably slack, you feel so clean and so strong and so idle, that whether you move or sit still, whatever you do is done with pride and a kingly sort of pleasure. You fall in talk with any one, wise or foolish, drunk or sober. And it seems as if a hot walk purged you, more than of anything else, of all narrowness and pride, and left curiosity to play its part freely, as in a child or a man of science. You lay aside all your own hobbies, to watch provincial humours develop themselves before you, now as a laughable farce, and now grave and beautiful like an old tale.

Or perhaps you are left to your own company for the night, and surly weather imprison you by the fire. You may remember how Burns, numbering past pleasures, dwells upon the hours when he has been 'happy thinking.' It is a phrase that may well perplex a poor modern, girt about on every side by clocks and chimes, and haunted, even at night, by flaming dial-plates. For we are all so busy, and have so many far-off projects to realize, and castles in the fire to turn into solid habitable mansions on a gravel soil, that we can find no time for pleasure trips into the Land of Thought and among the Hills of Vanity. Changed times, indeed, when we must sit all night, beside the fire, with folded hands; and a changed world for most of us, when we find we can pass the hours without discontent, and be happy thinking. We are in such haste to be doing, to be writing, to be gathering gear, to make our voice audible a moment in the derisive silence of eternity, that we forget that one thing, of which these are but the parts – namely, to live.

I travel not to go anywhere, but to go.
I travel for travel's sake. The great affair is to move.
ROBERT LOUIS STEVENSON

GREAT BRITAIN

☆ ☆ ☆

You lean from the window, your last pipe reeking whitely into the darkness, your body full of delicious pains, your mind enthroned in the seventh circle of content; when suddenly the mood changes, the weather-cock goes about, and you ask yourself one question more: whether, for the interval, you have been the wisest philosopher or the most egregious of donkeys? Human experience is not yet able to reply; but at least you have had a fine moment, and looked down upon all the kingdoms of the earth. And whether it was wise or foolish, to-morrow's travel will carry you body and mind, into some different parish of the infinite.

(From *Walking Tours* published in *Virginibus Puerisque and other papers;*
C. Kegan Paul, London, 1881)

Now shall I walk or shall I ride?
'Ride,' Pleasure said; 'Walk,' Joy replied.
WILLIAM HENRY DAVIES

Walking his best thoughts into existence, 1847

SØREN KIERKEGAARD

The philosopher Kierkegaard had a strange isolated childhood, kept at home by his father and made to walk around the rooms of the house each day noting everything he could see, rather than playing outside. Walking and thinking eventually became inseparable for him and as an adult he regularly walked the streets of Copenhagen, observing and contemplating. Any interruption would destroy the stream of thought, though, as he notes in this letter to his sister-in-law, Jette (Henriette).

But enough of this. I was sorry that I could not say goodbye to you; I hope that this little note by means of which I say goodbye will find you as well as I found you on my arrival.

Do not on any account cease to take pleasure in walking: I walk every day to preserve my well-being and walk away from every sickness; I have walked my best thoughts into existence, and I know of no thought so heavy that one cannot walk away from it. Even if one so pursued one's health that it always remained one step ahead I would still say: walk! It is quite obvious that by walking one always gets as close as possible to good health, even if one never completely attains it – but by sitting still, and the longer one sits still, the nearer will ill-health draw. Only in the motion of exercise are health and salvation to be found. If anyone denies that motion exists, then I do like Diogenes: I walk. If anyone denies that health is to be found in motion, then I walk away from all morbid objections. Thus if you go on walking, all will go well enough.

And in the country you have all the advantages; you are not able to be stopped even before you have safely emerged from the gateway, nor are you exposed to being intercepted on your way home. I recall exactly what happened to me some time ago, and what has indeed happened to me several times. I had been walking for an hour and a half, had done a good deal of thinking, and thanks to the motion I had grown agreeably relaxed. What happiness, and as you may imagine, what care I took to bring my happiness safely home, if possible. Thus I hurry along; with downcast eyes I steal, so to speak, through the streets. Confident of having the right of way I count on there being no need for looking up (how easily one is caught just when looking up – in order to escape), and thus hurrying along with my bliss on the sidewalk (for the prohibition against carrying anything on the sidewalk does not apply to blisses, which lighten one's burden) I run directly into a man who is always suffering from ill-health and who therefore walks with downcast eyes and, spiteful because of his ill-health, thinks that he need not look up even when he does not have the right of way. I was stopped. It was a distinguished gentleman who now honoured me with a conversation. Thus everything was lost. The conversation finished, there was only one thing for me to do: instead of walking home to walk again.

(From *Søren Kierkegaard*, from a letter to Henriette Kierkegaard, 1847)

Walking in the Rain, 1846

BAYARD TAYLOR

In his Coast to Coast Walk: A Pictorial Guide, *Alfred Wainwright says 'There's no such thing as bad weather, only unsuitable clothing.' Bayard Taylor believes that rain can sometimes even enhance a walk ...*

As we passed out the eastern gate, the workmen were busy near the city, making an embankment for the new railroad to Heilbroun, and we were obliged to wade through half a mile of mud. Finally the road turned to the left over a mountain, and we walked on in the rain, regardless of the touching entreaties of an omnibus-driver, who felt a great concern for our health, especially as he had two empty seats. There is a peculiarly agreeable sensation in walking in a storm, when the winds sweep by and the

Some people walk in the rain, others just get wet.
ROGER MILLER

rain-drops rattle through the trees, and the dark clouds roll past just above one's head. It gives a dash of sublimity to the most common scene. If the rain did not finally soak through the boots, and if one did not lose every romantic feeling in wet garments, I would prefer storm to sunshine, for visiting some kinds of scenery. You remember, we saw the North Coast of Ireland and the Giant's Causeway in stormy weather, at the expense of being completely drenched, it is true; but our recollections of that wild day's journey are as vivid as any event of our lives – and the name of the Giant's Causeway calls up a series of pictures as terribly sublime as any we would wish to behold.

(From *Views A-Foot; Europe Seen with Knapsack and Staff;*
Wiley & Putnam, New York, 1846)

CONTINENTAL EUROPE

First Night Out, 1902

HILAIRE BELLOC

Perhaps best known for his comic poems published as Cautionary Tales for Children, *Hilaire Belloc was also a historian and politician with a strong Catholic faith. Born in France but educated and eventually naturalised in Britain, he was always an ardent walker.*

In 1902, visiting Toul, the village of his birth, he made a vow at the local church to 'go to Rome on Pilgrimage and see all Europe which the Christian Faith has saved; and I said, 'I will start from the place where I served in arms for my sins; I will walk all the way and take advantage of no wheeled thing; I will sleep rough and cover thirty miles a day, and I will hear Mass every morning; and I will be present at high Mass in St Peter's on the Feast of St Peter and St Paul.''

I chose the decline of the day for setting out, because of the great heat a little before noon and four hours after it. Remembering this, I planned to walk at night and in the mornings and evenings, but how this design turned out you shall hear in a moment.

I had, in a small bag or pocket slung over my shoulder, a large piece of bread, half a pound of smoked ham, a sketch-book, two

Nationalist papers, and a quart of the wine of Brûlé – which is the most famous wine in the neighbourhood of the garrison, yet very cheap.

☆   ☆   ☆

The peasants sat outside their houses in the twilight accepting the cool air; every one spoke to me as I marched through, and I answered them all, nor was there in any of their salutations the omission of good fellowship or of the name of God. Saving with one man, who was a sergeant of artillery on leave, and who cried out to me in an accent that was very familiar and asked me to drink; but I told him I had to go up into the forest to take advantage of the night, since the days were so warm for walking. As I left the last house of the village I was not secure from loneliness, and when the road began to climb up the hill into the wild and the trees I was wondering how the night would pass.

☆   ☆   ☆

It was full night when I had reached a vague clearing in the woods, right up on the height of that flat hill. This clearing was called 'The Fountain of Magdalen'. I was so far relieved by the broader sky of the open field that I could wait and rest a little, and there, at last, separate from men, I thought of a thousand things. The air was full of midsummer, and its mixture of exaltation and fear cut me off from ordinary living. I now understood why our religion has made sacred this season of the year; why we have, a little later, the night of St John, the fires in the villages, and the old perception of fairies dancing in the rings of the summer grass. A general communion of all things conspires at this crisis of summer against us reasoning men that should live in the daylight, and something fantastic possesses those who are foolish enough to watch upon such nights. So I, watching, was cut off. There were huge, vague summits, all wooded, peering above the field I sat in, but they merged into a confused horizon. I was on a high plateau, yet I felt myself to be alone with the immensity that properly belongs to plains alone. I saw the stars, and remembered how I had looked up at them on just such a night when I was close to the Pacific, bereft of friends and possessed with soli-

These boots are made for walkin'
And that's just what they'll do...
NANCY SINATRA, *THESE BOOTS ARE MADE FOR WALKIN'*

CONTINENTAL EUROPE

tude. There was no noise; it was full darkness. The woods before and behind me made a square frame of silence, and I was enchased here in the clearing, thinking of all things.

Then a little wind passed over the vast forests of Lorraine. It seemed to wake an indefinite sly life proper to this seclusion, a life to which I was strange, and which thought me an invader. Yet I heard nothing. There were no adders in the long grass, nor any frogs in that dry square of land, nor crickets on the high part of the hill; but I knew that little creatures in league with every nocturnal influence, enemies of the sun, occupied the air and the land about me; nor will I deny that I felt a rebel, knowing well that men were made to work in happy dawns and to sleep in the night, and everything in that short and sacred darkness multiplied my attentiveness and my illusion. Perhaps the instincts of the sentry, the necessities of guard, come back to us out of the ages unawares during such experiments. At any rate the night oppressed and exalted me. Then I suddenly attributed such exaltation to the need of food.

'If we must try this bookish plan of sleeping by day and walking by night,' I thought, 'at least one must arrange night meals to suit it.'

I therefore, with my mind still full of the forest, sat down and lit a match and peered into my sack, taking out therefrom bread and ham and chocolate and Brûlé wine. For seat and table there was a heathery bank still full of the warmth and savour of the last daylight, for companions these great inimical influences of the night which I had met and dreaded, and for occasion or excuse there was hunger. Of the Many that debate what shall be done with travellers, it was the best and kindest Spirit that prompted me to this salutary act. For as I drank the wine and dealt with the ham and bread, I felt more and more that I had a right to the road; the stars became familiar and the woods a plaything. It is quite clear that the body must be recognized and the soul kept in its place, since a little refreshing food and drink can do so much to make a man.

On this repast I jumped up merrily, lit a pipe, and began singing, and heard, to my inexpressible joy, some way down the

CONTINENTAL EUROPE

When I see people on the street, I look at how they walk. It's like a signature, a fingerprint.
MIKHAIL BARYSHNIKOV

road, the sound of other voices. They were singing that old song of the French infantry which dates from Louis XIV, and is called 'Auprès de ma blonde'.

☆ ☆ ☆

I had now come some twelve miles from my starting-place, and it was midnight. The plain, the level road (which often rose a little), and the dank air of the river began to oppress me with fatigue. I was not disturbed by this, for I had intended to break these nights of marching by occasional repose, and while I was in the comfort of cities – especially in the false hopes that one got by reading books – I had imagined that it was a light matter to sleep in the open. Indeed, I had often so slept when I had been compelled to it in Manoeuvres, but I had forgotten how essential was a rug of some kind, and what a difference a fire and comradeship could make. Thinking over it all, feeling my tiredness, and shivering a little in the chill under the moon and the clear sky, I was very ready to capitulate and to sleep in bed like a Christian at the next opportunity. But there is some influence in vows or plans that escapes our power of rejudgement. All false calculations must be paid for, and I found, as you will see, that having said I would sleep in the open, I had to keep to it in spite of all my second thoughts.

I passed one village and then another in which everything was dark, and in which I could waken nothing but dogs, who thought me an enemy, till at last I saw a great belt of light in the fog above the Moselle. Here there was a kind of town or large settlement where there were ironworks, and where, as I thought, there would be houses open, even after midnight. I first found the old town, where just two men were awake at some cooking work or other. I found them by a chink of light streaming through their door; but they gave me no hope, only advising me to go across the river and try in the new town where the forges and the ironworks were. 'There,' they said, 'I should certainly find a bed.'

I crossed the bridge, being now much too weary to notice anything, even the shadowy hills, and the first thing I found was a lot of waggons that belonged to a caravan or fair. Here some

When you walk ten hours, eleven hours a day by yourself, you are doing a walking meditation.
SHIRLEY MACLAINE

men were awake, but when I suggested that they should let me sleep in their little houses on wheels, they told me it was never done; that it was all they could do to pack in themselves; that they had no straw; that they were guarded by dogs; and generally gave me to understand (though without violence or unpoliteness) that I looked as though I were the man to steal their lions and tigers. They told me, however, that without doubt I should find something open in the centre of the workmen's quarter, where the great electric lamps now made a glare over the factory.

I trudged on unwillingly, and at the very last house of this detestable industrial slavery, a high house with a gable, I saw a window wide open, and a blonde man smoking a cigarette at a balcony. I called to him at once, and asked him to let me a bed. He put to me all the questions he could think of. Why was I there? Where had I come from? Where (if I was honest) had I intended to sleep? How came I at such an hour on foot? and other examinations. I thought a little what excuse to give him, and then, determining that I was too tired to make up anything plausible, I told him the full truth; that I had meant to sleep rough, but had been overcome by fatigue, and that I had walked from Toul, starting at evening. I conjured him by our common Faith to let me in. He told me that it was impossible, as he had but one room in which he and his family slept, and assured me he had asked all these questions out of sympathy and charity alone. Then he wished me good-night, honestly and kindly, and went in.

By this time I was very much put out, and began to be angry. These straggling French towns give no opportunity for a shelter. I saw that I should have to get out beyond the market gardens, and that it might be a mile or two before I found any rest. A clock struck one. I looked up and saw it was from the belfry of one of those new chapels which the monks are building everywhere, nor did I forget to curse the monks in my heart for building them. I cursed also those who started smelting works in the Moselle valley; those who gave false advice to travellers; those who kept lions and tigers in caravans, and for a small sum I would have cursed the whole human race, when I saw that my bile had hurried me out of the street well into the countryside, and that above

side bar: CONTINENTAL EUROPE

From walking: something; from sitting: nothing.
BULGARIAN PROVERB

me, on a bank, was a patch of orchard and a lane leading up to it. Into this I turned, and, finding a good deal of dry hay lying under the trees, I soon made myself an excellent bed, first building a little mattress, and then piling on hay as warm as a blanket.

I did not lie awake (as when I planned my pilgrimage I had promised myself I would do), looking at the sky through the branches of trees, but I slept at once without dreaming, and woke up to find it was broad daylight, and the sun ready to rise. Then, stiff and but little rested by two hours of exhaustion, I took up my staff and my sack and regained the road.

(From *The Path to Rome*; George Allen, London, 1902)

Excelsior, 1841

HENRY WADSWORTH LONGFELLOW

The title and refrain in this poem by Longfellow (1807-82) is said to have been inspired by the motto on the state seal of New York, meaning 'onward and upward'. That appears to be what drives the young traveller here to continue, despite all warnings.

The shades of night were falling fast,
As through an Alpine village passed
A youth, who bore, 'mid snow and ice,
A banner with the strange device,
   Excelsior!

His brow was sad; his eye beneath,
Flashed like a falchion from its sheath,
And like a silver clarion rung
The accents of that unknown tongue,
   Excelsior!

In happy homes he saw the light
Of household fires gleam warm and bright;
Above, the spectral glaciers shone,
And from his lips escaped a groan,
   Excelsior!

We don't think about pilgrimage in this country. We don't think about meditation. The idea of taking a six-week walk

'Try not the Pass!' the old man said;
'Dark lowers the tempest overhead,
The roaring torrent is deep and wide!'
And loud that clarion voice replied,
    Excelsior!

'Oh stay,' the maiden said, 'and rest
Thy weary head upon this breast! '
A tear stood in his bright blue eye,
But still he answered, with a sigh,
    Excelsior!

'Beware the pine-tree's withered branch!
Beware the awful avalanche!'
This was the peasant's last Good-night,
A voice replied, far up the height,
    Excelsior!

At break of day, as heavenward
The pious monks of Saint Bernard
Uttered the oft-repeated prayer,
A voice cried through the startled air,
    Excelsior!

A traveller, by the faithful hound,
Half-buried in the snow was found,
Still grasping in his hand of ice
That banner with the strange device,
    Excelsior!

There in the twilight cold and gray,
Lifeless, but beautiful, he lay,
And from the sky, serene and far,
A voice fell like a falling star,
    Excelsior!

(From *Supplement to the Courant, Connecticut Courant, Vol VII No 2, Jan 22,* 1842)

CONTINENTAL EUROPE

**is totally foreign to most Americans. But it's probably exactly
what we need.** EMILIO ESTEVEZ

Athens, 1829

Thomas Alcock

Thomas Alcock (1801-66) visits Athens at the time when it was still under the control of Turkey and considers whether or not to take home a monumental souvenir. Engravings of this monument, also known as the Choragic Monument, were already in circulation in England. Lord Elgin later tried, unsuccessfully, to purchase it along with the Elgin Marbles.

Athens is, indeed, most interesting to every traveller; whether he wish to contemplate the finest ancient ruins in the world, which even the most savage battles, and the unparalleled events of a war of extermination have spared, as if barbarity itself had a respect for their antiquity; or whether, in looking at the ruined city, he delights to revel in the idea that, at some future moment, she may once more become the school of the sculptor, the historian, and the philosopher.

The few monuments of past grandeur standing amid a mass of ruin, as if saved by magic, – the wretched huts of some Albanian soldiers, – a paltry bazaar, – and five or six tolerable dwellings, in which the Bey and the chief officers reside, form the exact state of Athens in 1829. So divided, however, was the interest excited in the fallen city, that whilst I was making a tour of the ancient walls with Sir W. Gells' itinerary in my hand, my companion, who had served with the Greek army under General Church, was absorbed in contemplating the position of the Turks while besieging the citadel, and examining the tambours thrown up at one time by the Greeks, and at another by the Turks.

We were now, indeed, on the site of the ancient wall of the city, near the Philopappus, on the ground, perhaps, from whence Sylla besieged and took Athens, 86 B. C. ; where the Venetians attacked and took it in 1687; and where the Turks made an assault in 1827. Near this spot is the Pnyx of the Pisistratidae. The identical rostrum from whence, perhaps, Demosthenes and Pericles may have addressed the Athenians, still remains perfect. It is a platform, nearly square, cut out of the solid rock, and has a commanding view over the city, as if to give effect to the eloquence, of which it was the most distinguished theatre in the world. This interesting relic carried me back more completely to the flourishing era of Greece, than any other object I had met with in the course of my tour.

Having, with some difficulty, clambered over large heaps of rubbish, we were amply repaid by a specimen of the most beautiful Corinthian order, the tomb of Lysicrates, better known as the lantern of Demosthenes. Its preservation seemed miraculous, but was owing to the protection of a monastery, in which it had been immured; and the revolution which destroyed the asylum happily spared the precious monument it contained. Under the impression that this, as well as other valuable remains, would, according to the assurance of the Turks, fall a prey to their vengeance before they left Athens, I ventured to ask the Bey if he would permit me to have it carried away, rather than suffer it to risk being destroyed; adding that the stones were of no value, and that I could send him European articles of much more use to him. He replied, in the plenitude of his delight at the prospect I held out of presents, that I might have it, and that if it were worth millions still he should he happy it were so well disposed of.

For the moment I was willing to entertain hopes that I might be able to rescue this beautiful ruin from entire destruction, and procure for the British Museum a specimen of Grecian architecture, such as it has not at present in its collection; but, on reflection, I found it would be difficult to remove, without material injury, a mass of about the weight of eight tons ; and I was not anxious to incur the reproach of despoiling Greece of that which, perhaps, may still be an object of pride to her in her dawn of freedom, in spite of the determination of the Turks. I therefore abandoned this project, which, like many other resolves, gave a momentary delight in anticipation, although it was never destined to be realized.

We regretted not being able to ascend the Acropolis, although we had as good an external view of the Parthenon, from the city, as we could have desired. The Turks are so distrustful they would not permit any one to enter the citadel: they pretend-

CONTINENTAL EUROPE

ed, in their boastful manner, that they had provisions and ammunition for three years, and would never give up the city, although the Sultan commanded it.

(From *Travels in Russia, Persia, Turkey, and Greece, in 1828-9*, 1831)

My body must be exercised to make my judgement active, 1765

JEAN JACQUES ROUSSEAU

Born in 1712 in Switzerland and moving to France when he was 16, Rousseau was a philosopher and political theorist whose writings inspired the leaders of the French Revolution. In Paris he was one of a group of intellectuals that included Denis Diderot who was eventually imprisoned for his sacrilegious writings. Rousseau said that it was while walking that some of his greatest ideas came to him and, indeed, it was on a walk from Paris to visit Diderot in prison in Vincennes that he had the 'illumination' that modern progress had not advanced the majority of the population but held them back.

What I most regret, is not having kept a journal of my travels, being conscious that a number of interesting details have slipped my memory; for never did I exist so completely, never live so thoroughly, never was so much myself, if I dare use the expression, as in those journeys made on foot. Walking animates and enlivens my spirits; I can hardly think when in a state of inactivity; my body must be exercised to make my judgment active.

The view of a fine country, a succession of agreeable prospects, a free air, a good appetite, and the health I gained by walking; the freedom of inns, and the distance from everything that can make me recollect the dependence of my situation, conspire to free my soul, and give boldness to my thoughts, throwing me, in a manner, into the immensity of beings, where I combine, choose and appropriate them to my fancy, without constraint or fear. I dispose of all nature as I please; my heart wandering from object to object, approximates and unites with those that please it, is surrounded by charming images, and becomes intoxicated with delicious sensations. If, attempting to render

I've taken to long-distance walking as a means of dissolving the mechanised matrix which compresses the space-time continuum, and decouples human from physical geography.

these permanent, I am amused in describing to myself, what glow of colouring, what energy of expression, do I give them! – It has been said, that all these are to be found in my works, though written in the decline of life. Oh! had those of my early youth been seen, those made during my travels, composed, but never written! – Why did I not write them? will be asked; and why should I have written them? I may answer. Why deprive myself of the actual charm of my enjoyments to inform others what I enjoyed? What to me were readers, the public, or all the world, while I was mounting the empyrean. Besides, did I carry pens, paper and ink with me? Had I recollected all these, not a thought would have occurred worth preserving. I do not foresee when I shall have ideas; they come when they please, and not when I call for them; either they avoid me altogether, or rushing in crowds, overwhelm me with their force and number. Ten volumes a day would not suffice barely to enumerate my thoughts; how then should I find time to write them? In stopping, I thought of nothing but a hearty dinner; on departing, of nothing but a charming walk; I felt that a new paradise awaited me at the door, and eagerly leaped forward to enjoy it.

Never did I experience this so feelingly as in the perambulation I am now describing. On coming to Paris, I had confined myself to ideas which related to the situation I expected to occupy there. I had rushed into the career I was about to run, and should have completed it with tolerable éclat, but it was not that my heart adhered to. Some real beings obscured my imagined ones – Colonel Godard and his nephew could not keep pace with a hero of my disposition. Thank Heaven, I was soon delivered from all these obstacles, and could enter at pleasure into the wilderness of chimeras, for that alone remained before me, and I wandered in it so completely that I several times lost my way; but this was no misfortune, I would not have shortened it, for, feeling with regret, as I approached Lyons, that I must again return to the material world, I should have been glad never to have arrived there.

One day, among others, having purposely gone out of my way to take a nearer view of a spot that appeared delightful, I

CONTINENTAL EUROPE

So this isn't walking for leisure – that would be merely frivolous, or even for exercise – which would be tedious ....
WILL SELF, *PSYCHOGEOGRAPHY*

was so charmed with it, and wandered round it so often, that at length I completely lost myself, and after several hours' useless walking, weary, fainting with hunger and thirst, I entered a peasant's hut, which had not indeed a very promising appearance, but was the only one I could discover near me. I thought it was here, as at Geneva, or in Switzerland, where the inhabitants, living at ease, have it in their power to exercise hospitality. I entreated the countryman to give me some dinner, offering to pay for it: on which he presented me with some skimmed milk and coarse barley-bread, saying it was all he had. I drank the milk with pleasure, and ate the bread, chaff and all; but it was not very restorative to a man sinking with fatigue. The countryman, who watched me narrowly, judged the truth of my story by my appetite, and presently (after having said that he plainly saw I was an honest, good-natured young man, and did not come to betray him) opened a little trap door by the side of his kitchen, went down, and returned a moment after with a good brown loaf of pure wheat, the remains of a well-flavoured ham, and a bottle of wine, the sight of which rejoiced my heart more than all the rest: he then prepared a good thick omelet, and I made such a dinner as none but a walking traveller ever enjoyed.

When I again offered to pay, his inquietude and fears returned; he not only would have no money, but refused it with the most evident emotion; and what made this scene more amusing, I could not imagine the motive of his fear. At length, he pronounced tremblingly those terrible words, 'Commissioners,' and 'Cellar-rats,' which he explained by giving me to understand that he concealed his wine because of the excise, and his bread on account of the tax imposed on it; adding, he should be an undone man, if it was suspected he was not almost perishing with want. What he said to me on this subject (of which I had not the smallest idea) made an impression on my mind that can never be effaced, sowing seeds of that inextinguishable hatred which has since grown up in my heart against the vexations these unhappy people suffer, and against their oppressors. This man, though in easy circumstances, dare not eat the bread gained by the sweat of his brow, and could only escape destruction by exhibiting an out-

I frequently tramped eight or ten miles through the deepest snow to keep an appointment with a beech-tree,

ward appearance of misery! – I left his cottage with as much indignation as concern, deploring the fate of those beautiful countries, where nature has been prodigal of her gifts, only that they may become the prey of barbarous exactors.

(From *Confessions*; Aldus Society, London, 1903)

Mountain-climbing in Switzerland, 1880
MARK TWAIN

Mark Twain (born Samuel Langhorne Clemens, 1835-1910), travelling in the Alps, decides to 'find out what this much-talked-of mountain-climbing was like, and how one should go about it'. He soon sets off with Harris, his companion (a fictional character based on his friend Joseph Twichell) but they find adventure enough just on the path approaching the mountains...

A great and priceless thing is a new interest! How it takes possession of a man! how it clings to him, how it rides him! I strode onward from the Schwarenbach hostelry a changed man, a reorganized personality. I walked into a new world, I saw with new eyes. I had been looking aloft at the giant show-peaks only as things to be worshipped for their grandeur and magnitude, and their unspeakable grace of form; I looked up at them now, as also things to be conquered and climbed. My sense of their grandeur and their noble beauty was neither lost nor impaired; I had gained a new interest in the mountains without losing the old ones. I followed the steep lines up, inch by inch, with my eye, and noted the possibility or impossibility of following them with my feet. When I saw a shining helmet of ice projecting above the clouds, I tried to imagine I saw files of black specks toiling up it roped together with a gossamer thread.

We skirted the lonely little lake called the Daubensee, and presently passed close by a glacier on the right – a thing like a great river frozen solid in its flow and broken square off like a wall at its mouth. I had never been so near a glacier before.

☆   ☆   ☆

Right under us a narrow ledge rose up out of the valley, with

CONTINENTAL EUROPE

or a yellow birch, or an old acquaintance among the pines.
H.D. THOREAU

a green, slanting, bench-shaped top, and grouped about upon this green-baize bench were a lot of black and white sheep which looked merely like oversized worms. The bench seemed lifted well up into our neighborhood, but that was a deception – it was a long way down to it.

We began our descent, now, by the most remarkable road I have ever seen. It wound its corkscrew curves down the face of the colossal precipice – a narrow way, with always the solid rock wall at one elbow, and perpendicular nothingness at the other. We met an everlasting procession of guides, porters, mules, litters, and tourists climbing up this steep and muddy path, and there was no room to spare when you had to pass a tolerably fat mule. I always took the inside, when I heard or saw the mule coming, and flattened myself against the wall.

☆   ☆   ☆

There was one place where an eighteen-inch breadth of light masonry had been added to the verge of the path, and as there was a very sharp turn here, a panel of fencing had been set up there at some time, as a protection. This panel was old and gray and feeble, and the light masonry had been loosened by recent rains. A young American girl came along on a mule, and in making the turn the mule's hind foot caved all the loose masonry and one of the fence-posts overboard; the mule gave a violent lurch inboard to save himself, and succeeded in the effort, but that girl turned as white as the snows of Mont Blanc for a moment.

The path was simply a groove cut into the face of the precipice; there was a four-foot breadth of solid rock under the traveler, and four-foot breadth of solid rock just above his head, like the roof of a narrow porch; he could look out from this gallery and see a sheer summitless and bottomless wall of rock before him, across a gorge or crack a biscuit's toss in width – but he could not see the bottom of his own precipice unless he lay down and projected his nose over the edge. I did not do this, because I did not wish to soil my clothes.

Every few hundred yards, at particularly bad places, one came across a panel or so of plank fencing; but they were always

CONTINENTAL EUROPE

old and weak, and they generally leaned out over the chasm and did not make any rash promises to hold up people who might need support. There was one of these panels which had only its upper board left; a pedestrianizing English youth came tearing down the path, was seized with an impulse to look over the precipice, and without an instant's thought he threw his weight upon that crazy board. It bent outward a foot! I never made a gasp before that came so near suffocating me. The English youth's face simply showed a lively surprise, but nothing more. He went swinging along valleyward again, as if he did not know he had just swindled a coroner by the closest kind of a shave.

☆　　☆　　☆

This dreadful path has had its tragedy. Baedeker, with his customary over terseness, begins and ends the tale thus:

'The descent on horseback should be avoided. In 1861 a Comtesse d'Herlincourt fell from her saddle over the precipice and was killed on the spot.'

We looked over the precipice there, and saw the monument which commemorates the event. It stands in the bottom of the gorge, in a place which has been hollowed out of the rock to protect it from the torrent and the storms. Our old guide never spoke but when spoken to, and then limited himself to a syllable or two, but when we asked him about this tragedy he showed a strong interest in the matter. He said the Countess was very pretty, and very young – hardly out of her girlhood, in fact. She was newly married, and was on her bridal tour. The young husband was riding a little in advance; one guide was leading the husband's horse, another was leading the bride's.

The old man continued:

'The guide that was leading the husband's horse happened to glance back, and there was that poor young thing sitting up staring out over the precipice; and her face began to bend downward a little, and she put up her two hands slowly and met it – so, – and put them flat against her eyes – so – and then she sank out of the saddle, with a sharp shriek, and one caught only the flash of a dress, and it was all over.'

CONTINENTAL EUROPE

Even when I am writing I usually take a break around lunchtime and go for a little walk to clear out my head.
PATRICIA CORNWELL

Then after a pause:

'Ah, yes, that guide saw these things – yes, he saw them all. He saw them all, just as I have told you.'

After another pause:

'Ah, yes, he saw them all. My God, that was me. I was that guide!'

This had been the one event of the old man's life; so one may be sure he had forgotten no detail connected with it. We listened to all he had to say about what was done and what happened and what was said after the sorrowful occurrence, and a painful story it was.

When we had wound down toward the valley until we were about on the last spiral of the corkscrew, Harris's hat blew over the last remaining bit of precipice – a small cliff a hundred or hundred and fifty feet high – and sailed down toward a steep slant composed of rough chips and fragments which the weather had flaked away from the precipices. We went leisurely down there, expecting to find it without any trouble, but we had made a mistake, as to that. We hunted during a couple of hours – not because the old straw hat was valuable, but out of curiosity to find out how such a thing could manage to conceal itself in open ground where there was nothing left for it to hide behind. When one is reading in bed, and lays his paper-knife down, he cannot find it again if it is smaller than a saber; that hat was as stubborn as any paper-knife could have been, and we finally had to give it up; but we found a fragment that had once belonged to an opera-glass, and by digging around and turning over the rocks we gradually collected all the lenses and the cylinders and the various odds and ends that go to making up a complete opera-glass. We afterward had the thing reconstructed, and the owner can have his adventurous lost-property by submitting proofs and paying costs of rehabilitation. We had hopes of finding the owner there, distributed around amongst the rocks, for it would have made an elegant paragraph; but we were disappointed.

(From *A Tramp Abroad*; American Publishing Co, Hartford, Conn, 1880)

A bear, however hard he tries, grows tubby without exercise. A.A. MILNE, *WINNIE-THE-POOH*

The Simplon Pass, 1790

WILLIAM WORDSWORTH

Wordsworth (1770-1850) hiked over this 2006-metre pass on 17th August 1790 with his friend, Robert Jones, following the route that is now known as the Stockalper Trail, a mule track named after the baron who controlled trade over the pass at that time.

                    Brook and road
Were fellow-travellers in this gloomy Pass,
And with them did we journey several hours
At a slow step. The immeasurable height
Of woods decaying, never to be decayed,
The stationary blasts of waterfalls,
And in the narrow rent, at every turn,
Winds thwarting winds bewildered and forlorn,
The torrents shooting from the clear blue sky,
The rocks that muttered close upon our ears,
Black drizzling crags that spake by the wayside
As if a voice were in them, the sick sight
And giddy prospect of the raving stream,
The unfettered clouds and region of the heavens,
Tumult and peace, the darkness and the light
Were all like workings of one mind, the features
Of the same face, blossoms upon one tree,
Characters of the great Apocalypse,
The types and symbols of Eternity,
Of first and last, and midst, and without end.

(From *William Wordsworth – Poems*, 1845)

CONTINENTAL EUROPE

I can't tell you how oppressive it is
never to be able to go outdoors.
ANNE FRANK, *THE DIARY OF A YOUNG GIRL*

The Panic that Haunts High Places, 1902
HILAIRE BELLOC

On his pilgrimage to Rome, Belloc reaches a deep gorge and must choose between a long walk down into the gorge and up the other side or a short cut over a frighteningly high bridge ...

The gorge of the Doubs, of which I said a word or two above, is of that very rare shape which isolates whatever may be found in such valleys. It turns right back upon itself, like a very narrow U, and thus cannot by any possibility lead any one anywhere; for though in all times travellers have had to follow river valleys, yet when they come to such a long and sharp turn as this, they have always cut across the intervening bend ...

I thought a good deal about what the Romans did to get through the Mont Terrible, and how they negotiated this crook in the Doubs (for they certainly passed into Gaul through the gates of Porrentruy, and by that obvious valley below it). I decided that they probably came round eastward by Delemont. But for my part, I was on a straight path to Rome, and as that line lay just along the top of the river bend I was bound to take it.

Now outside St Ursanne, if one would go along the top of the river bend and so up to the other side of the gorge, is a kind of subsidiary ravine – awful, deep, and narrow – and this was crossed, I could see, by a very high railway bridge.

Not suspecting any evil, and desiring to avoid the long descent into the ravine, the looking for a bridge or ford, and the steep climb up the other side, I made in my folly for the station which stood just where the railway left solid ground to go over this high, high bridge. I asked leave of the stationmaster to cross it, who said it was strictly forbidden, but that he was not a policeman, and that I might do it at my own risk. Thanking him, therefore, and considering how charming was the loose habit of small uncentralized societies, I went merrily on to the bridge, meaning to walk across it by stepping from sleeper to sleeper. But it was not to be so simple. The powers of the air, that hate to have their kingdom disturbed, watched me as I began.

I roamed the countryside searching for answers to things I did not understand.
LEONARDO DA VINCI

I had not been engaged upon it a dozen yards when I was seized with terror.

I have much to say further on in this book concerning terror: the panic that haunts high places and the spell of many angry men. This horrible affection of the mind is the delight of our modern scribblers; it is half the plot of their insane 'short stories', and is at the root of their worship of what they call 'strength', a cowardly craving for protection, or the much more despicable fascination of brutality. For my part I have always disregarded it as something impure and devilish, unworthy of a Christian. Fear I think, indeed, to be in the nature of things, and it is as much part of my experience to be afraid of the sea or of an untried horse as it is to eat and sleep; but terror, which is a sudden madness and paralysis of the soul, that I say is from hell, and not to be played with or considered or put in pictures or described in stories. All this I say to preface what happened, and especially to point out how terror is in the nature of a possession and is unreasonable.

For in the crossing of this bridge there was nothing in itself perilous. The sleepers lay very close together – I doubt if a man could have slipped between them; but, I know not how many hundred feet below, was the flashing of the torrent, and it turned my brain. For the only parapet there was a light line or pipe, quite slender and low down, running from one spare iron upright to another. These rather emphasized than encouraged my mood. And still as I resolutely put one foot in front of the other, and resolutely kept my eyes off the abyss and fixed on the opposing hill, and as the long curve before me was diminished by successive sharp advances, still my heart was caught half-way in every breath, and whatever it is that moves a man went uncertainly within me, mechanical and half-paralysed. The great height with that narrow unprotected ribbon across it was more than I could bear.

I dared not turn round and I dared not stop. Words and phrases began repeating themselves in my head as they will under a strain: so I know at sea a man perilously hanging on to the tiller makes a kind of litany of his instructions. The central part was passed, the three-quarters; the tension of that enduring

CONTINENTAL EUROPE

Climb the mountain so you can see the world, not so the world can see you.
ANON

effort had grown intolerable, and I doubted my ability to complete the task. Why? What could prevent me? I cannot say; it was all a bundle of imaginaries. Perhaps at bottom what I feared was sudden giddiness and the fall –

At any rate at this last supreme part I vowed one candle to Our Lady of Perpetual Succour if she would see that all went well, and this candle I later paid in Rome; finding Our Lady of Succour not hung up in a public place and known to all, as I thought She would be, but peculiar to a little church belonging to a Scotchman and standing above his high altar. Yet it is a very famous picture, and extremely old.

Well, then, having made this vow I still went on, with panic aiding me, till I saw that the bank beneath had risen to within a few feet of the bridge, and that dry land was not twenty yards away. Then my resolution left me and I ran, or rather stumbled, rapidly from sleeper to sleeper till I could take a deep breath on the solid earth beyond.

I stood and gazed back over the abyss; I saw the little horrible strip between heaven and hell – the perspective of its rails. I was made ill by the relief from terror. Yet I suppose railway-men cross and recross it twenty times a day. Better for them than for me!

(From *The Path to Rome*; George Allen, London, 1902)

Ever wonder where you'd end up if you took your dog for a walk and never once pulled back on the leash?
ROBERT BRAULT

ASIA

3

Crossing a Human Causeway, 1833
REV W.M. THOMSON

William McClure Thomson (1806-94) was an American Protestant missionary who arrived in Beirut in 1833. He established a college there which formed the basis of the American University in Beirut. The account of his travels in the region, The Land and the Book, *was one of the best-selling books of the 19th century. Revisiting the Chapel of the Cross in Jerusalem, Thomson recalls his first visit and the novel way in which he was led across the crowds inside it.*

My introduction to that church was totally different, and my first impressions were most unhappy. On the 6th of April, 1833 I arrived from Ramleh much fatigued, but, as an important ceremony was going forward in the church, I hastened thither at once. The whole edifice was crowded with pilgrims from all parts of the world, and it was with difficulty that I followed my companion into the rotunda. There a priest who knew us came up, and, after inquiring about the news of the day, asked if we would be conducted into the interior of the Greek chapel, where the religious services were going on, and then summoning a Turkish cawâss, we began to move in that direction. To my amazement and alarm, the cawâss began to beat the crowd over the head, when down they crouched to the floor, and we walked over their prostrate bodies. There was no help for it; those behind, rising up, thrust us forwards. After proceeding some distance, we paused to take breath where the crowd was more dense and obstinate than usual, and I was seriously informed that there was the exact centre of the earth, and those obstinate pilgrims were bowing and kissing it. Finally we reach the altar at the east end without any serious injury to the living causeway which we had traversed, and I had time to look about me.

The scene throughout had all the interest of entire novelty. I was young, and just from America, and was seized with an almost irrepressible propensity to laugh. The noise was deafening, and there was not the slightest approximation to devotion visible, or even possible, so far as I could judge; while the attitudes, costumes, gestures, and sounds which met the eye and stunned the ear were infinitely strange and ludicrous. Such splendor, too, I had never seen. By the aid of numerous lamps, the whole church seemed to flash and blaze in burning gold. I stood near the altar, which was covered with cloth of gold, and decorated with censers, golden candlesticks, and splendid crucifixes.

(From *The Land and the Book*; Harper & Bros, New York, 1859)

A Jolly Evening in a Koutan, 1905

STEPHEN GRAHAM

Stephen Graham (1884-1975) was the son of the editor of the magazine Country Life *and was always a keen walker. During his lifetime he made many long journeys on foot, walking – or tramping as he often called it – being the best means to experience a country.*

I was at Kutais in the beginning of May, and I walked from that town two hundred miles across the Caucasus to Vladikavkaz, which I am told is a notable feat. It will certainly remain very notable in my mind, both in respect of the sights I saw and of the adventures I survived. I ascended from the Italian loveliness of Imeretia, where the wild fruit was already ripening in the forests, to the bleak and barren solitudes of Ossetia, where I had to plough my way through ten miles of waist-deep snow. I was attacked by roughs at Gurshevi and escaped from them only to lose myself on the Mamison Pass, where I found the road overswept by a twelve-feet drift of snow.

☆   ☆   ☆

... I dragged myself through a mile of 'slosh,' where a profusion of yellow water-lilies were growing, and for the best part of an hour I strove to find the road again. When I found it and followed

My father considered a walk among the mountains as the equivalent of churchgoing. ALDOUS HUXLEY

it I came rapidly to snow too soft and deep to pass; indeed, twenty yards in front the road was perfectly lost in the snow, unmarked by undulation or rift in the even whiteness.

I was desperate, but I felt sure there was a way, for I had heard of hillmen coming from Utsera, and had been even counselled to wait for a companion there. I resolved to get a shepherd to show me the way, and with that in view climbed awkwardly downhill to the turfy region, where a flock was browsing. Yes, there was a way – one quite different from the road; an Ossetine shepherd offered to show me for a shilling. I agreed on condition that he first gave me a glass of milk, for I was exhausted and had eaten nothing since morning. This man was friendly enough, but on consideration he thought it impossible to show me that night. I should have to wait until next morning. I might sleep with them in their koutan if I didn't mind the filth; they would make a bonfire and a big supper. His mate, Gudaev, would play the fiddle ; I could sing. He would roast two quails which Achmet had killed; they would all have a jolly evening, and to-morrow morning very early he would take me and show me the track. Very thankfully I agreed.

☆　　☆　　☆

Chekai and his companion shepherds living in the koutan were clad in rags that were extremely dirty, their faces red, unshaven and wild, and their feet and legs bare, except of dirt. They were extremely apologetic. 'You are clean,' said Gudaev, 'but God has given us to work in filth, as you see, but we are men and Christian Ossetines.' I put them at their ease with a smile and went to inspect the koutan. It was an extensive dwelling, for the most part dug out of the mountain side. The walls were made of boulders plastered wind-tight with stable filth, the roof of pine branches, peat and hay. There were no windows, and so the whole had no light beyond what came in at the door, or from the hole in the roof; but what light there was sufficed to show that the house was divided by fences into a number of compartments for the reception of horses, cows, sheep and goats.

One of these compartments, in the shelter of a ponderous rock, was the shepherds' own room. Three bits of fir trunk made the seats, and between these trunks and the walls were the beds of hay where they slept. Under the rock the red-grey embers of last night's fire still smouldered. I went in and sat down, being tired and cold after my wanderings in the wet snow on the pass. Chekai and his companions milked the cows, brought in the horses and the sheep, separated and drove into separate pens the rams, the ewes and the lambs, so that the dark koutan became full of the cries of animals. I myself assisted in the separating of the sheep, for Chekai, who had asked my name, kept calling out, 'Stepan, come here,' 'Stepan, go there,' and I was fain to obey.

Achmet brought me the two quails he had killed, and showed me them with pride. He must have been a sure marksman with stones, and I thought with some ruefulness of my recent encounter when I had been somewhat in the position of the poor quails, but I said nothing. Gudaev, having milked the cows, took up the business of hacking firewood out of a tough pine log. In his intervals of rest he brought armfuls of wet branches and put them on the fire. I was given a wooden basinful of fresh milk, which Achmet had strained through hay before giving me. Presently the animals were all housed and a bonfire made up on the rude hearth. Clouds had crawled once again into the evening sky, there was a flash of lightning and a long roll of thunder ; the dancing hailstones rushed down, and following them thick, soft, flaky snow.

I was glad I had not tried to cross the pass that night. It was very dark, and the wet wood was filling the koutan with smoke, but Chekai, who had cut up a great number of little sticks, made a brilliant illumination by setting fire to them. They had a contrivance of tin about three feet from the ground, and in this they burned the resinous pine splinters for hours. At length the brushwood burst into flame and dried and caught the thicker branches; in half an hour we had a roaring big fire. Gudaev hung a large iron pot over it and boiled water; Chekai settled down to pluck the quails; Achmet prepared to make bread. When the water had boiled Chekai informed me they would make copatchka. Achmet took maize flour, salt and milk and boiling water, and kneaded a dough into flat cakes about the size of soup plates. Gudaev stood

Walking is the exact balance between spirit and humility.
GARY SNYDER

them on end in front of the fire, and toasted them first one side and then the other. When they were done he buried them under the grey-red ashes and left them to cook.

This done, he took from a wooden peg in the mud of the wall an iron violin with two strings, and commenced a tune of that sighing and moaning and shrieking style characteristic of Caucasian music. Chekai sang, and all the while plucked the little quails. When the birds had been quite disfeathered, singed and cleaned, the shepherd transfixed them together on a stake and toasted them at the fire. Achmet filled up the pot over the fire with milk, flour and salt, thereby preparing soup. I had fallen back asleep when suddenly Chekai called out, 'Stepan, get up and eat!' This I was not loth to do, and in a minute behold me tasting for the first time hot copatchka and roast quail. It must be said the bird was tasty though it was small. The milk soup made my teeth dance, it was so hot.

Chekai began a conversation. 'What are the English Christians or Mahometans?' asked he. 'Is England far away? Where does it lie?' I replied that it was four or five thousand versts to the north-west. Chekai whistled. 'Beyond the mountains?' said he. 'And have they such poor and dirty people there? Look how poor I am, look how I'm dressed.'

'I expect you're not so poor as you look,' said I.

'The owners of the sheep must pay you well, but you leave the money in the village with your wife and family, or your mother.'

The shepherd frowned and then grinned. I had apparently hit on the truth.

The time came to make an end of the feast and lie down to sleep. They gave me the best place between a fir plank and a sheep fence close to the hot embers. I covered myself entirely up in my travelling-bed, and was secure in that both from vermin and from dirt. The three others disposed themselves in different parts of the smoky cavern and began to snore horribly. I slept heavily.

At dawn, through custom, I awoke. Chekai was already stirring and had gathered fresh wood for the fire. He warned me it

ASIA

Great things are done when men and mountains meet;
This is not done by jostling in the street.
WILLIAM BLAKE, *NOTEBOOKS* (1793)

was necessary to hurry if he was to show me the track, for he had much work to do. I showed immediate alacrity. The weather seemed promising, and I was full of hope that I should reach the other side of the mountains in time for breakfast. We had a ten minutes' parley over money. Chekai wasn't quite sure that he couldn't hold me up to ransom *à la Hadgi Stavros*. But he was eventually content to receive half-a-crown, together with the present of a pretty water-jar I had bought a week before in Georgia, and which he coveted. In exchange for the water-jar he presented me with his staff, which was stout and long and served me better in the long run than I could have guessed. I ought to have taken another meal of copatchka and milk before starting. A bottle of vodka in my pocket would not have been amiss. I did not dream that after two hours walking my heart would be beating so violently through exertion that I should fear to perish in the snow.

(From *A vagabond in the Caucasus, with some notes of his experiences among the Russians*, John Lane, London & New York, 1911, © Stephen Graham)

Lost in Armenia, 1828

THOMAS ALCOCK

Thomas Alcock (1801-66) was a politician who had his account of his adventurous travels in Russia, Turkey, Persia and Greece self published in 1830.

On the side of Ararat is a hermitage, supposed to be Noah's habitation on his descent, and the first in the world. This venerable mountain has a most imposing appearance; in addition to its peculiar form, it rises from a champaign country, and appears to much greater effect from there being no other eminences in the vicinity of it, on the side from which we viewed it.

On leaving Erivan we had intended to visit the seven churches of Guerni, cut out of the solid rock; but on this occasion our first disaster befel us, and we failed in the object of our expedition. Having set out late, night overtook us before we could expect to arrive at the village, and as it snowed the whole day,

There may be more to learn from climbing the same mountain a hundred times than by climbing a hundred different mountains. RICHARD NELSON

our guide had every excuse for mistaking the road. We had observed him for some time looking from right to left, as if he was out of his latitude, and he at length acknowledged he had lost his way. For many long hours we endeavoured by loudly hallooing to make ourselves heard, but our vociferations were vain: we were creeping into a chimney in despair of a better place of rest, when, about one o'clock in the morning, we thought we discerned the bark of a watch dog; having advanced towards the sound, we found in a ruined church our baggage, for the men with the mules had fortunately found their way there also, and an immense flock of sheep, and we began now to understand the cause of our misfortune. The poor guide, whom we had abused for stupidity, had directed his course properly enough; but the village had been demolished when the Russians had passed through in their pursuit of the Persians in the late war, and nothing remained but the stone walls of this welcome church, which now formed an asylum for sheep, and which from the darkness of the night we should not have discovered but for the shepherd's dog. No hotel, however well provided and sumptuous, was ever so welcome as this old church, which afforded at least a shelter against a continued fall of snow.

We soon made a fire, and an attack upon the provision-basket made amends for previous cold and hunger. We congratulated ourselves that we had gained experience, which might afterwards be of use to us, not to place too much reliance upon the existence of towns, and run the risk of being benighted in a similar manner. As the villages are universally built of earth, they disappear altogether from time to time, and so complete is the destruction, that it is no exaggeration to say that the mud walls once fallen, soon unite with the ground, and the plough goes over them, leaving not a vestige to be seen.

There seems to be nothing to remind the traveller in Armenia of its ancient kingdom, and, like Poland, and several other states, now under the dominion of Russia, (the crowns of most of which are deposited among the regalia at Moscow,) it is scarcely known to exist.

(From *Travels in Russia, Persia, Turkey, and Greece, in 1828-9*, 1831)

**It isn't the mountain ahead that wears you out;
it's the grain of sand in your shoe.**
ROBERT W. SERVICE

Easter in Jerusalem, 1833
Rev W.M. Thomson

During Easter, in his walk around Jerusalem, Thomson visits the Church of the Sepulchre to witness the Ceremony of the Holy Fire.

Dean Stanley gives an admirable account of it, but he says that, 'considering the place, the time, and the intention of the professed miracle,' it is 'probably the most offensive imposture to be found in the world.' The dean witnessed the ceremony of the Holy Fire in 1853. I will describe it as I saw it just twenty years before his visit. The ceremonies vary somewhat on different occasions, but are always substantially the same.

Knowing that this was the grand event of Easter-week, and that the desire to participate in it had drawn multitudes to the church, I expected a great crowd of pilgrims, and therefore went early; but the edifice was already densely packed. Not only were the rotunda and adjoining chapels below filled with eager and expectant crowds, but so, also, was every niche and corner, gallery, balcony, window, and possible standing-place, rising rank above rank along the walls of the rotunda. The Chapel of the Sepulchre loomed up from amidst the mass of pilgrims who stood or sat about; and around them a lane was formed by the soldiers stationed to keep back the crowds pressing from behind, and to preserve order. Upon entering, I was startled by the ringing zulagît of the women, echoing through the grand dome in a manner most surprising. I had never heard it before. It is a shrill âh-wê-hâ, long-sustained quivering and trilling into an endless lâ-lâ-lâ-lâ-lee, once heard never forgotten, and which every Arab woman can execute with more or less proficiency. I have heard it thousands of times since that day, at weddings and on festive occasions, but never by such a multitude of excited and jubilant performers.

We had secured places on an elevated platform at the northern side of the rotunda, and directly in front of the aperture through which the Holy Fire was to make its appearance, and from there had the entire boisterous scene below us in full view.

Earth and sky, woods and fields, lakes and rivers, the mountain and the sea, are excellent schoolmasters, and teach

It seemed to be the belief that, unless some one ran round the Sepulchre a certain number of times, the fire would not issue from the hole. Accordingly, individual pilgrims would run round, breaking through the lines, until stopped by the soldiers. Frequently one man, fastening upon the shoulders of another, like the Old Man in the story of Sinbad the Sailor, would compel him to run round the circle, until, jumping off, he would be succeeded by another. Occasionally four stout men, standing face to face, would form a hollow square. Upon their shoulders four others were hoisted, and this living column would start off round the Sepulchre at a perilous rate – those above swinging their Greek cap or Arab tarboush, as the case might be – singing, shouting, clapping their hands, waving handkerchiefs, and twisting their bodies into the most absurd contortions. These exhibitions would wake up the echoes of the zulagît to deafening screams. At times the whole circle between the troops would join in procession, and a man would be carried round feigning death, borne upon men's shoulders, the people following, cursing the Jews and praising themselves.

☆　☆　☆

I witnessed this strange scene for four hours, the crowd increasing constantly from about noon until the fire appeared. The crush around the aperture whence the light was to issue was tremendous, as by this time there were thousands of pilgrims within the building besides the spectators. Some Greek sailors, from a man-of-war anchored at Jaffa, had stationed themselves at the aperture, and others, particularly the men of Bethlehem, endeavored to force them away. They yelled, and swore, and fought, and had not the soldiers frequently rushed in and forcibly separated the combatants, serious mischief would have occurred.

At half-past twelve a bell rang, and I was informed that the governor of the city had arrived. He is responsible, and must always be present on these occasions to preserve order. Soldiers paraded round the Sepulchre continually, and often had to use their merciless whips.

About one o'clock the grand clerical procession commenced to move round the Sepulchre with large banners, having painted

ASIA

some of us more than we can ever learn from books.
JOHN LUBBOCK

on them representations of the various scenes in the Passion of the Saviour. Soldiers marched before, and, beating the people on the head, cleared the way. Following the banners came the priests and bishops, resplendent in their canonicals of purple and gold, some swinging censers, others chanting the appointed anthems. An aged bishop, surrounded by a picked band, closed the procession. Having with much difficulty encircled the tomb three times, the bishop entered the Sepulchre alone. Then there was for a few moments a profound and expectant silence.

At length a light shone in the aperture, a bundle of prepared tapers was thrust in, and quickly withdrawn all ablaze. Instantly the whole vast edifice rang with exultant shouts. The scrambling and fighting for the light that succeeded beggars all description. The people were frantic – leaping, dancing, shouting, and swinging their burning tapers in the air. A swift horseman was despatched to carry the sacred fire to the Greek church at Bethlehem. Gradually the Holy Fire spread from hand to hand, till at last the entire rotunda, from pavement to gallery, balcony and window, blazed with thousands of lighted tapers. When the light reached us, a person sitting next to me, passing his flaming tapers under his chin and over his face, declared that it was pure light from heaven, and would not burn. I thrust a bit of paper into them, and it ignited immediately. 'Don't look at that,' he exclaimed – 'don't look at that; it burns because you have no faith:' and again he passed them over his face and under his chin, but this time so leisurely that his beard was decidedly singed: and yet such is the strength of this strange delusion, that even this man asserted most vehemently that it was divine light, and not ordinary fire.

I was amazed to witness the reverence with which this Holy Fire is regarded. Not only do the people pass it over their faces many times, open their clothes – both men and women – and thrust the lighted tapers into their bosoms, but they gather the smoke in their hands, and rub themselves as if with a precious perfume. They fumigate extra garments, brought for the purpose, and finally carry the offensive ends of the candles to their distant homes, for the relief of the sick and the consolation of the dying.

It is not talking but walking that will bring us to heaven.
MATTHEW HENRY

My companion asked a priest who sat near him what all the noise and confusion we had just witnessed meant. 'Joy, joy,' he replied, 'But what kind of joy?' 'Joy in the Lord,' said he, laughing, in evident confusion at the absurdity of the thing.

There was not the least appearance of religious reverence during the entire ceremony, and to me the spectacle was extremely humiliating; and when I remembered that this was the most imposing exhibition of the Greek religion which the Mohammedan or the Turk ever see – though some of their ceremonies are equally offensive – I could no longer be surprised that they despise the name and faith of such Christians, and call them dogs and idolaters. I was here the next year, when several hundred pilgrims were crushed to death in their frantic efforts to burst open the door and escape from the suffocating fumes within, caused by the sudden kindling of an unusual multitude of tapers. The celebrated Ibrahim Pasha, of Egypt, with his staff, was present on that occasion, and was with much difficulty rescued by his guard. But I need not describe that awful scene. We have, perhaps, dwelt too long upon this subject – in no way an agreeable one – but it is well I suppose, to know what dreadful results ignorant fanaticism and designing priestcraft may bring about in this world.

(From *The Land and the Book;* Harper & Bros, New York, 1859)

A Passage to India, 1924
E.M. FORSTER

Dr Aziz has organised a lavish trip to the Malabar Caves to impress his English friend Mrs Moore and her younger companion Adele Quested who is to marry Mrs Moore's son, Ronny. At the first caves Mrs Moore feels faint and decides to wait while the others walk on.

Miss Quested and Aziz and a guide continued the slightly tedious expedition. They did not talk much, for the sun was getting high. The air felt like a warm bath into which hotter water is trickling constantly, the temperature rose and rose, the boulders said, 'I am alive,' the small stones answered, 'I am almost alive.'

Between the chinks lay the ashes of little plants. They meant to climb to the rocking-stone on the summit, but it was too far, and they contented themselves with the big group of caves. *En route* for these, they encountered several isolated caves, which the guide persuaded them to visit, but really there was nothing to see; they lit a match, admired its reflection in the polish, tested the echo and came out again. Aziz was 'pretty sure they should come on some interesting old carvings soon', but only meant he wished there were some carvings. His deeper thoughts were about the breakfast. Symptoms of disorganization had appeared as he left the camp. He ran over the menu: an English breakfast, porridge and mutton chops, but some Indian dishes to cause conversation, and pan afterwards. He had never liked Miss Quested as much as Mrs Moore, and had little to say to her, less than ever now that she would marry a British official.

Nor had Adela much to say to him. If his mind was with the breakfast, hers was mainly with her marriage. Simla next week, get rid of Antony, a view of Tibet, tiresome wedding bells, Agra in October, see Mrs Moore comfortably off from Bombay – the procession passed before her again, blurred by the heat, and then she turned to the more serious business of her life at Chandrapore. There were real difficulties here – Ronny's limitations and her own – but she enjoyed facing difficulties, and decided that if she could control her peevishness (always her weak point), and neither rail against Anglo-India nor succumb to it, their married life ought to be happy and profitable. She mustn't be too theoretical; she would deal with each problem as it came up, and trust to Ronny's common sense and her own. Luckily, each had abundance of common sense and good will.

But as she toiled over a rock that resembled an inverted saucer, she thought, 'What about love?' The rock was nicked by a double row of footholds, and somehow the question was suggested by them. Where had she seen footholds before? Oh yes, they were the pattern traced in the dust by the wheels of the Nawab Bahadur's car. She and Ronny – no, they did not love each other.

'Do I take you too fast?' inquired Aziz for she had paused, a doubtful expression on her face. The discovery had come so suddenly that she felt like a mountaineer whose rope had broken. Not to love the man one's going to marry! Not to find out till this moment! Not even to have asked oneself the question until now! Something else to think out. Vexed rather than appalled, she stood still, her eyes on the sparkling rock. There was esteem and animal contact at dusk, but the emotion that links them was absent. Ought she to break her engagement off? She was inclined to think not – it would cause so much trouble to others; besides, she wasn't convinced that love is necessary to a successful union. If love is everything, few marriages would survive the honeymoon. 'No, I'm all right, thanks', she said, and, her emotions well under control, resumed the climb, though she felt a bit dashed. Aziz held her hand, the guide adhered to the surface like a lizard and scampered about as if governed by a personal centre of gravity.

'Are you married, Dr Aziz?' she asked, stopping again, and frowning.

'Yes, indeed, do come and see my wife' – for he felt it more artistic to have his wife alive for a moment.

'Thank you', she said absently.

'She is not at Chandrapore just now.'

'And have you children?'

'Yes, indeed, three,' he replied in firmer tones.

'Are they a great pleasure to you?' 'Why, naturally, I adore them,' he laughed.

'I suppose so.' What a handsome little Oriental he was, and no doubt his wife and children were beautiful too, for people usually get what they already possess. She did not admire him with any personal warmth, for there was nothing of the vagrant in her blood, but she guessed he might attract women of his own race and rank, and she regretted that neither she nor Ronny had physical charm. It does make a difference in a relationship – beauty, thick hair, a fine skin. Probably this man had several wives – Mohammedans always insist on their full four, according to Mrs Turton. And having no one else to speak to on that eternal rock, she gave rein to the subject of marriage and said in

I'm sure I should be myself were I once among the heather on those hills. EMILY BRONTË, *WUTHERING HEIGHTS*

her honest, decent, inquisitive way: 'Have you one wife or more than one?'

The question shocked the young man very much. It challenged a new conviction of his community, and new convictions are more sensitive than old. If she had said, 'Do you worship one god or several?' he would not have objected. But to ask an educated Indian Moslem how many wives he has – appalling, hideous! He was in trouble how to conceal his confusion. 'One, one in my own particular case,' he spluttered, and let go of her hand. Quite a number of caves were at the top of the track, and thinking, 'Damn the English even at their best,' he plunged into one of them to recover his balance. She followed at her leisure, quite unconscious that she had said the wrong thing. and not seeing him, she also went into a cave, thinking with half her mind 'sight-seeing bores me', and wondering with the other half about marriage.

(From *A Passage to India*, Edward Arnold (London) & Harcourt Brace (New York), 1924, © E.M. Forster)

The Salt March, 1930
Mahatma Gandhi

In 1930 Gandhi led a symbolic march from his ashram near Ahmedabad for 240 miles to the coast to gather salt in an act of civil disobedience, protesting against British rule in India. It started the nation-wide campaign of non-violent civil disobedience known as satyagraha. *Tens of thousands of Indians joined him and almost 60,000 were arrested, Gandhi among them.*

Dear Mr. Gandhi,
His Excellency the Viceroy desires me to acknowledge your letter of the 2nd March. He regrets to learn that you contemplate a course of action which is clearly bound to involve violation of the law and danger to the public peace.
Yours very truly, G. Cunningham, Private Secretary

The reader is familiar with this reply. He will note, too, that it begs the question; and if further justification were needed, this stereotyped reply affords it. On bended knees I asked for bread and I have received stone instead.

I find it a lot healthier for me to be someplace where I can go outside in my bare feet.
James Taylor

It was open to the Viceroy to disarm me by freeing the poor man's salt, tax on which costs him five annas per year or nearly three days' income. I do not know outside India anyone who pays to the State Rs. 3 per year, if he earns Rs. 360 during that period. It was open to the Viceroy to do many other things except sending the usual reply. But the time is not yet. He represents a nation that does not easily give in, that does not easily repent. Entreaty never convinces it. It readily listens to physical force. It can witness with bated breath a boxing match for hours without fatigue. It can go mad over a football match in which there may be broken bones. It goes into ecstasies over blood-curdling accounts of war. It will listen also to mute resistless suffering. It will not part with the millions it annually drains from India in reply to any argument, however convincing. The Viceregal reply does not surprise me.

But I know that the salt tax has to go and many other things with it, if my letter means what it says. Time alone can show how much of it was meant.

The reply says I contemplate a course of action which is clearly bound to involve violation of the law and danger to the public peace. In spite of the forest of books containing rules and regulations, the only law that the nation knows is the will of the British administrators, the only public peace the nation knows is the peace of a public prison. India is one vast prison house. I repudiate this law and regard it as my sacred duty to break the mournful monotony of the compulsory peace that is choking the heart of the nation for want of free vent.

☆　　☆　　☆

[Speech at prayer meeting, Sabarmati Ashram, 12 March 1930] God willing, we shall set out exactly at 6.30. Those joining the march should all be on the spot at 6.20. If our first step is pure, all our subsequent steps will be good and pure. As Manilal is joining us, I would say something for his benefit. He should not join just because he is my son though he cannot help being my son, nor can I forget that I am his father.

We who are setting out with a great responsibility on our heads – we the Ashram inmates – have but one capital. We can boast of no learning. We who took certain vows and pledged ourselves to the Ashram way of life ought to adhere to those vows scrupulously. The seventy-two men joining the march should once again read the Ashram rules and think whether or not they should join the march. Those inmates of the Ashram who have any dependents will not be able to draw money from the Ashram for them. None should join the struggle with that hope. This fight is no public show; it is the final struggle – a life-and-death struggle. If there are disturbances, we may even have to die at the hands of our own people. Even in that case, we shall have made our full contribution to the *satyagraha* struggle. We have constituted ourselves the custodians of Hindu-Muslim unity. We hope to become the representatives of the poorest of the poor, the lowest of the low and the weakest of the weak. If we do not have the strength for this, we should not join the struggle. For my part I have taken no pledge not to return here, but I do ask you to return here only as dead men or as winners of swaraj. Chhaganlal Joshi will not be able to run up here if Dhiru falls ill. Even if the Ashram is on fire, we will not return. Only those may join, who have no special duty to their relatives. The marchers have vowed to follow life-long poverty and to observe *brahmacharya* for life. They leave here with the determination to observe *brahmacharya* and will remain faithful to that determination. The man who always follows truth and always proclaims what he does is a brave man. Anyone who deceives others is not brave. I cannot speak to anyone privately for I have not a minute to spare. Though addressing myself to Manilal particularly, I say this to all.

We are entering upon a life-and-death struggle, a holy war; we are performing an all-embracing sacrifice in which we wish to offer ourselves as oblation. If you prove incapable, the shame will be mine, not yours. You too have in you the strength that God has given me. The Self in us all is one and the same. In me it has awakened; in others, it has awakened partially.

(From *Young India*, 12-3-1930 and the manuscript of Mahadev Desai's Diary, both in *The Collected Works of Mahatma Gandhi*, Vol XLIII)

It is impossible to walk rapidly and be unhappy.
MOTHER TERESA

Himalayan Vistas, 1853

BAYARD TAYLOR

Taylor visits Landowr (near Mussoorie) to admire the tallest mountains in the world, three years before Everest had been correctly located and measured by the Great Trigonometrical Survey of India.

I had now reached the summit of the second range of the Himalayas, 8,000 feet above the sea. The cottage where we were quartered was perched on a narrow shelf, scooped out of the side of the mountain. From the balcony where I sat, I could have thrown a stone upon the lowest house in the place. For the first time in several weeks, the thermometer was above freezing-point, and the snows with which the roof was laden poured in a shower from the eaves. Around me the heights were bleak and white and wintry, but down the gorge below me – far down in its warm bed – I could see the evergreen vegetation of the Tropics. Buried to the knees in a snow-drift, I looked upon a palm-tree, and could almost smell the blossoms of the orange-bowers in a valley where frost never fell. It was like sitting at the North Pole, and looking down on the Equator.

I had a letter to Mr. Woodside, an American Missionary who lived upon the highest point of Landowr, and Mr. Keone and I visited him during the afternoon. We had still half a mile to climb before reaching the summit of the mountain, which I found to be a sharp, serrated crest, not more than ten yards in breadth. Mr. Woodside's house commands a view of both sides of the Sub-Himalayas; and a natural mound beside it has been ascertained, by measurement, to be the loftiest spot in this part of the range. The house and mound were purchased by a benevolent Philadelphian as a sanitarium for Missionaries – a thing much needed by that class. I suggested to Mr. Woodside the propriety of planting a tall flagstaff on the mound, and running up the national colors on certain anniversaries.

The view from this point best repaid me for my journey to the hills. The mound on which we stood was conical, and only twenty feet in diameter at the summit. The sides of the mountain fell

ASIA

Just living is not enough ... one must have sunshine, freedom, and a little flower.
HANS CHRISTIAN ANDERSEN

away so suddenly that it had the effect of a tower, or of looking from the mast-head of a vessel. In fact, it might be called the 'main truck' of the Sub-Himalayas. The sharp comb, or ridge, of which it is the crowning point, has a direction of north-west to south-east (parallel to the great Himalayan range), dividing the panorama into two hemispheres, of very different character. To the north, I looked into the wild heart of the Himalaya – a wilderness of barren peaks, a vast jumble of red mountains, divided by tremendous clefts and ravines, of that dark indigo hue, which you sometimes see on the edge of a thunder-cloud – but in the back-ground, towering far, far above them, rose the mighty pinnacles of the Gungootree, the Junmootre, the Budreenath, and the Kylas, the heaven of Indra, where the Great God, Mahadeo, still sits on his throne, inaccessible to mortal foot. I was fifty miles nearer these mountains than at Roorkhee, where I first beheld them, and with the additional advantage of being mounted on a footstool, equal to one third of their height. They still stood immeasurably above me, so cold, and clear, and white, that, without knowledge to the contrary, I should have said that they were not more than twenty miles distant. Yet, as the crow flies, a line of seventy miles would scarce have reached their summits!

☆   ☆   ☆

There is a peculiarity in the structure of the Himalayas, of which I had not heard, until I visited them. At their north-western extremity, on the frontiers of Cashmere and Afghanistan, the lower or Sub-Himalayas are lofty, and so separated by deep valleys from the higher or snowy range, as almost to form a parallel chain. As we proceed eastward, however, the relative height of the two ranges gradually changes. The peaks of the Upper Himalayas increase in height, while those of the Sub-Himalayas decrease. A little to the east of the Dhoon, the Siwalik Hills cease entirely. The Sub-Himalayas gradually dwindle away toward Nepaul, becoming more narrow and broken as they approach the termination of the chain. Dwalagheri, in the main Himalayan chain, once supposed to be the highest mountain in the world, is in Nepaul. But further to the east, is Chumalari, which is still

I like girls who like the countryside, put on walking boots and can bend with the wind a bit. If you're going to live with me,

higher, and recent measurements have discovered that another peak, still further eastward, in the former province of Sikim, is higher than Chumalari. This regular increase of altitude in the Himalayas, as you proceed eastward, is very curious. The height of Dwalagheri is estimated at 27,000 feet; Chumalari, a little more than 28,000, and the third peak, the name of which I forget, fully 30,000 feet!

☆　☆　☆

There is a temple near the source of the Ganges, but owing to the danger and difficulty of the journey, comparatively few pilgrims reach it. The air of the mountain is pure, fresh and invigorating, and the Paharrees are said to be both physically and mentally superior to the inhabitants of the plains. Mr. D'Aguilar considered them as a strikingly honest and faithful race. Owing to the difficulty of procuring subsistence, and the necessity of restricting the increase of population, Polyandry has existed among them from time immemorial. The woman and her husbands live together harmoniously, and the latter contribute each an equal share to the support of the children. Among these people the saying will particularly apply: 'It's a wise child that knows its own father.' Another of their customs is still more singular. Their ideas of hospitality compel them to share not only their food, but their connubial right with the stranger, and no insult is so great as a refusal to accept it. While in Landowr, I saw several of them walking bare-legged through the snow, which troubled them as little as it would a horse. They were handsome, muscular fellows, with black eyes, ivory teeth and a ruddy copper complexion.

I spent the afternoon with Mr. Woodside, and at sunset went again upon the mound, to witness the illumination of the Himalayas. Although there were clouds in the sky, the range was entirely obscured, and the roseate glare of its enormous fields of snow, shooting into flame-shaped pinnacles, seemed lighted up by the conflagration of a world. It was a spectacle of surpassing glory, but so brief, that I soon lost the sense of its reality.

I was called, however, to witness another remarkable phe-

ASIA

nomenon. Turning from the fading hills, I looked to the south. The Dehra Dhoon was buried under a sea of snow-white clouds, which rolled and surged against each other, sinking and rising, like the billows of an agitated sea. Where we stood, the air was pure and serene; but far away, over that cloudy deluge – which soon tossed its waves above the peaks of the Siwalik Hills – more than a hundred miles away – and high in air, apparently, ran a faint blue horizon-line, like that of the sea. It was the great plain of Hindostan, but so distant that the delusion was perfect. The great white billows rose, and rose, whirling and tossing as they poured into the clefts of the hills, till presently we stood as on a little island in the midst of a raging sea. Still they rose, disclosing enormous hollows between their piled masses; cliffs, as of wool, toppled over the cavities; avalanches slid from the summits of the ridges and slowly fell into the depths; and as I looked away for many a league over the cloudy world, there was motion everywhere, but not a sound. The silence was awful, and as the vast mass arose, I felt an involuntary alarm, lest we should be overwhelmed. But to our very feet the deluge came, and there rested. Its spray broke against the little pinnacle whereon we stood, but the billows kept their place. It was as if a voice had said: ' Thus far shalt thou come, and no further: and here shall thy proud waves be stayed.'

(From *A visit to India, China, and Japan in the year 1853*; G.P. Putnam, New York, 1855)

Conquering Everest, 1953

EDMUND HILLARY

John Hunt (1910-98) led the expedition to climb Mt Everest that included Edmund Hillary and Tenzing Norgay who made the summit together on 29th May 1953. The news of their success reached London on the day of Queen Elizabeth's coronation. In Hunt's book, Hillary wrote the chapter about the final climb ...

At 4 am it was very still. I opened the tent door and looked far out across the dark and sleeping valleys of Nepal. The icy peaks below us were glowing clearly in the early morning light and

It is not the mountain we conquer but ourselves.
EDMUND HILLARY

Tenzing pointed out the Monastery of Thyangboche, faintly visible on its dominant spur 16,000 feet below us. It was an encouraging thought to realize that even at this early hour the Lamas of Thyangboche would be offering up devotions to their Buddhist Gods for our safety and well-being.

We started up our cooker, and in a determined effort to prevent the weaknesses arising from dehydration we drank large quantities of lemon juice and sugar, and followed this with our last tin of sardines on biscuits. I dragged our oxygen sets into the tent, cleaned the ice off them and then completely rechecked and tested them. I had removed my boots, which had become a little wet the day before, and they were now frozen solid. Drastic measures were called for, so I cooked them over the fierce flame of the Primus and despite the very strong smell of burning leather managed to soften them up. Over our down clothing we donned our windproofs and on to our hands we pulled three pairs of gloves – silk, woollen and windproof.

At 6.30 am we crawled out of our tent into the snow, hoisted our 30 lb. of oxygen gear on to our backs, connected up our masks and turned on the valves to bring life-giving oxygen into our lungs. A few good deep breaths and we were ready to go. Still a little worried about my cold feet, I asked Tenzing to move off and he kicked a deep line of steps away from the rock bluff which protected our tent out on to the steep powder snow slope to the left of the main ridge. The ridge was now all bathed in sunlight and we could see our first objective, the South summit, far above us. Tenzing, moving purposefully, kicked steps in a long traverse back towards the ridge and we reached its crest just where it forms a great distinctive snow bump at about 28,000 feet.

☆   ☆   ☆

I had been cutting steps continuously for two hours, and Tenzing, too, was moving very slowly. As I chipped steps around still another corner, I wondered rather dully just how long we could keep it up. Our original zest had now quite gone and it was turning more into a grim struggle. I then realized that the ridge ahead, instead of still monotonously rising, now dropped sharply away, and far below I could see the North Col

Iron rusts from disuse; water loses its purity from stagnation ... even so does inaction sap the vigour of the mind.
LEONARDO DA VINCI

and the Rongbuk glacier. I looked upwards to see a narrow snow ridge running up to a snowy summit. A few more whacks of the ice-axe in the firm snow and we stood on top.

My initial feelings were of relief – relief that there were no more steps to cut – no more ridges to traverse and no more humps to tantalize us with hopes of success. I looked at Tenzing, and in spite of the balaclava, goggles and oxygen mask all encrusted with long icicles that concealed his face, there was no disguising his infectious grin of pure delight as he looked all around him. We shook hands and then Tenzing threw his arm around my shoulders and we thumped each other on the back until we were almost breathless. It was 11.30 am. The ridge had taken us two and a half hours, but it seemed like a lifetime. I turned off the oxygen and removed my set. I had carried my camera, loaded with colour film, inside my shirt to keep it warm, so I now produced it and got Tenzing to pose on top for me, waving his axe on which was a string of flags – United Nations, British, Nepalese and Indian.

(From *The Ascent of Everest*; Hodder & Stoughton, London, 1953, © John Hunt)

An Opium Trip, 1853
BAYARD TAYLOR

Travelling in China, having attempted to come to terms with Pigeon (Pidgin) English, Taylor walks along the river to the visit the Temple of Honan then, in the interests of research, visits an opium den.

Whoever first invented the 'pigeon English,' as it is called – the jargon used by foreigners in their intercourse with Chinese – deserves an immortality of ridicule. The jargon has now become so fixed, that it will take several generations to eradicate it. The Chinaman requires as much practice to learn it as he would to learn correct English, while the Englishman, in his turn, must pick it up as he would a new language. Fancy, for instance, a man going into one of the silverware shops in New China-street, and saying, 'My wantye two piece snuff-box: can secure?' when his meaning is simply – 'I want two snuff-boxes: can you get them?'

The less you carry the more you will see, the less you spend the more you will experience.
STEPHEN GRAHAM, *THE GENTLE ART OF TRAMPING*

To which A-Wing gravely answers: 'Can secure.' Or, another declaring: 'My no savey that pigeon' – which signifies in English: 'I don't understand the business.' If you make inquiries at a hotel, you must ask: 'What man have got top-side? ' (Who are up stairs?) and the Chinese servant will make answer: 'Two piece captain, one piece joss-man, have got.' (There are two captains and a clergyman.) It was some time before I could bring myself to make use of this absurd and barbarous lingo, and it was always very unpleasant to hear it spoken by a lady.

As far as sight-seeing is concerned, Canton has very little to offer the traveller, and I was so thoroughly surfeited with China that I made no effort to see more than the most prominent objects. Mr. Wells Williams and the Rev. Mr. Bonney were kind enough to accompany me through the Temple of Honan, on the opposite side of the river. This is a place of great sanctity, embracing within its bounds a well-endowed college of Boodhist priests. There are a number of temples, or rather shrines of the gods, standing within enclosed courts, which are shaded by large and venerable trees. We first passed through a portal, placed in advance, like the pylon of an Egyptian temple, with a colossal figure on each side, of the watchers or guardians of the edifice. With their distended abdomens, copper faces and fierce black eyeballs, they might very well have passed for Gog and Magog. The temples were massive square structures, with peaked roofs, containing colossal gilded statues of various divinities, most of whom were seated cross-legged, with their hands on their stomachs and a grin of ineffable good-humor on their faces. They were no doubt represented as having dined well, and therefore the more easily to be propitiated. We reached the main temple in time to witness the rites of the Boodhist priests. Numerous candles and 'joss-sticks' of sandal-wood were burning at the foot of the vast statues, and the shaven-headed priests, thirty or forty in number, walked solemnly in a circle around the open space before them, chanting their hymns. The character of the chants was very similar to some of those used in the Roman Catholic service, and there were other features in the ceremonies of the priests which showed the same resemblance. I believe this fact has been noticed by other travellers.

Meandering leads to perfection.
Lao Tzu

☆   ☆   ☆

On our way back to the river, we passed through the habitation of the priests, taking a look at their kitchens and refectories. A number of the younger brethren gathered around us, lusting strongly after the carnal gratification of cigars, and my whole stock was soon divided among them. Mr. Bonney took me to visit a former abbot, a man of much learning, who was then living in a quiet way, on a pension. He received us with much cordiality, and showed us his bachelor establishment of three rooms and a little garden, which were kept in great neatness and order. He was about sixty years of age, and his pale face, calm eye and high, retreating brow, spoke of a serene and studious life. In an inner chamber, however, I noticed one of those couches which are used by the opium-smokers, and the faint, subtle odor of the drug still hung about the furniture and the walls.

In spite of the penalties attached to it by Chinese law, the smoking of opium is scarcely a concealed practice at present. I have seen it carried on in open shops in Shanghai, where there are some streets which are never free from the sickening smell. It had always been my intention to make a trial of the practice, in order to learn its effects by personal experience, and being now on the eve of leaving China, I applied to a gentleman residing in Canton, to put me in the way of enjoying a pipe or two. He was well acquainted with a Chinaman who was addicted to the practice, and by an agreement with him, took me to his house one evening. We were ushered into a long room, with a divan, or platform about three feet high, at the further end. Several Chinamen were in the room, and one, stretched out on the platform, was preparing his pipe at a lamp. The host invited me to stretch myself opposite to him, and place my head upon one of those cane head-stools which serve the Chinese in lieu of pillows.

The opium-pipe is a bamboo stick, about two feet long, having a small drum inserted near the end, with an aperture in its centre. A piece of opium, about twice the size of a pin's head, is taken up on a slender wire and held in the flame of the lamp until it boils or bubbles up, when it is rolled into a cylindrical shape on the drum, by the aid of the wire. It loses its dark color by the heat-

A rainy day is the perfect time for a walk in the woods.
RACHEL CARSON

ing and becomes pale and soft. Having been sufficiently rolled, it is placed over the aperture, and the wire, after being thrust through its centre, to allow the air to pass into the pipe, is withdrawn. The pipe is then held to the flame, and as the opium burns, its fumes are drawn into the lungs by a strong and long-continued inspiration. In about half a minute the portion is exhausted, and the smoker is ready for a second pipe.

To my surprise I found the taste of the drug as delicious as its smell is disagreeable. It leaves a sweet, rich flavor, like the finest liquorice, upon the palate, and the gentle stimulus it communicates to the blood in the lungs, fills the whole body with a sensation of warmth and strength. The fumes of the opium are no more irritating to the windpipe or bronchial tubes, than common air, while they seem imbued with a richness of vitality far beyond our diluted oxygen. I had supposed that opium was smoked entirely for the purpose of mental exhilaration, and that to the smokers, as to many who intoxicate themselves with ardent spirits, there was no sensual gratification in the mere taste of the article. The reverse is undoubtedly the truth, and the practice, therefore, is doubly dangerous. Its victim becomes hopelessly involved in its fascinating illusions, and an awful death, such as I had witnessed not long before, is sure, sooner or later, to overtake him who indulges to excess. I have a pretty strong confidence in my own powers of resistance, but do not desire to make the experiment a second time.

Beyond the feeling of warmth, vigor and increased vitality, softened by a happy consciousness of repose, there was no effect, until after finishing the sixth pipe. My spirits then became joyously excited, with a constant disposition to laugh; brilliant colors floated before my eyes, but in a confused and cloudy way, sometimes converging into spots like the eyes in a peacock's tail, but oftenest melting into and through each other, like the hues of changeable silk. Had the physical excitement been greater, they would have taken form and substance, but after smoking nine pipes I desisted, through fear of subjecting myself to some unpleasant after-effect. Our Chinese host informed me that he was obliged to take twenty pipes in order to elevate his mind to

ASIA

There's something about the rhythm of walking, how, after about an hour and a half, the mind and body can't help getting in sync. BJORK

the pitch of perfect happiness. I went home feeling rather giddy, and became so drowsy, with slight qualms at the stomach, that I went to bed at an early hour. I had made an arrangement to walk around the walls of Canton the next morning, with Mr. Bonney, and felt some doubt as to whether I should be able to undertake it; but, after a deep and refreshing sleep, I arose at sunrise, feeling stronger and brighter than I had done for weeks past.

(From *A visit to India, China, and Japan in the year 1853*; G.P. Putnam, New York, 1855)

Among the Tibetans, 1889

ISABELLA BIRD

On her visit to Nubra in Ladakh, Isabella Bird (1831-1904) travels with a Buddhist monk, Gergan, and a Moravian missionary, Mr Redslob, whom she describes as 'a man of noble physique, a scholar and linguist ... (who had) ... devoted himself to the welfare of the Tibetan, and though his great aim was to Christianize them, he gained their confidence so thoroughly ... he was loved and welcomed everywhere.' Before the climb to visit the Monastery of Deskyid (Deskit), the party stays at Gergan's family home.

Our food in this hospitable house was simple: apricots, fresh, or dried and stewed with honey, sour milk, curds and cheese, sour cream, peas, beans, balls of barley dough, barley porridge, and 'broth of abominable things'. Chang, a dirty-looking beer made from barley, was offered with each meal, and tea frequently, but I took my own 'on the sly.' I have mentioned a churn as part of the 'furnishings' of the living-room. In Tibet the churn is used for making tea! I give the recipe. 'For six persons. Boil a teacupful of tea in three pints of water for ten minutes with a heaped dessert-spoonful of soda. Put the infusion into the churn with one pound of butter and a small tablespoonful of salt. Churn until as thick as cream.' Tea made after this fashion holds the second place to chang in Tibetan affections. The butter according to our thinking is always rancid, the mode of making it is uncleanly, and it always has a rank flavour from the goatskin in which it was kept. Its value is enhanced by age. I saw skins of it forty, fifty, and even

ASIA

The place where you lose the trail is not necessarily the place where it ends.
TOM BROWN

sixty years old, which were very highly prized, and would only be opened at some special family festival or funeral.

During the three days of our visits to Hundar both men and women wore their festival dresses, and apparently abandoned most of their ordinary occupations in our honour. The men were very anxious that I should be 'amused' and made many grotesque suggestions on the subject. 'Why is the European woman always writing or sewing?' they asked. 'Is she very poor, or has she made a vow?'

Visits to some of the neighbouring monasteries were eventually proposed, and turned out most interesting. The monastery of Deskyid, to which we made a three days' expedition, is from its size and picturesque situation the most imposing in Nubra. Built on a majestic spur of rock rising on one side 2,000 feet perpendicularly from a torrent, the spur itself having an altitude of 11,000 feet, with red peaks, snow-capped, rising to a height of over 20,000 feet behind the vast irregular pile of red, white, and yellow temples, towers, storehouses, cloisters, galleries, and balconies, rising for 300 feet one above another, hanging over chasms, built out on wooden buttresses, and surmounted with flags, tridents, and yaks' tails, a central tower or keep dominating the whole, it is perhaps the most picturesque object I have ever seen, well worth the crossing of the Shayok fords, my painful accident, and much besides. It looks inaccessible, but in fact can be attained by rude zigzags of a thousand steps of rock, some natural, others roughly hewn, getting worse and worse as they rise higher, till the later zigzags suggest the difficulties of the ascent of the Great Pyramid. The day was fearfully hot, 99 in the shade, and the naked, shining surfaces of purple rock with a metallic lustre radiated heat. My 'gallant grey' took me up half-way – a great feat – and the Tibetans cheered and shouted 'Sharbaz I' ('Well done!') as he pluckily leapt up the great slippery rock ledges.

After I dismounted, any number of willing hands hauled and helped me up the remaining horrible ascent, the rugged rudeness of which is quite indescribable. The inner entrance is a gateway decorated with a yak's head and many Buddhist emblems. High

ASIA

We have to walk in a way that we only print peace and serenity on the Earth. Walk as if you are kissing the Earth with your feet. THICH NHAT HANH

above, on a rude gallery, fifty monks were gathered with their musical instruments. As soon as the Kan-po or abbot, Punt-sog-sogman (the most perfect Merit), received us at the gate, the monkish orchestra broke forth in a tornado of sound of a most tremendous and thrilling quality, which was all but overwhelming, as the mountain echoes took up and prolonged the sound of fearful blasts on six-foot silver horns, the bellowing thunder of six-foot drums, the clash of cymbals, and the dissonance of a number of monster gongs. It was not music, but it was sublime. The blasts on the horns are to welcome a great personage, and such to the monks who despised his teaching was the devout and learned German missionary. Mr. Redslob explained that I had seen much of Buddhism in Ceylon and Japan, and wished to see their temples. So with our train of gopaa, zemindar, peasants, and muleteers, we mounted to a corridor full of lamas in ragged red dresses, yellow girdles, and yellow caps, where we were presented with plates of apricots, and the door of the lowest of the seven temples heavily grated backwards.

The first view, and indeed the whole view of this temple of Wrath or Justice, was suggestive of a frightful Inferno, with its rows of demon gods, hideous beyond Western conception, engaged in torturing writhing and bleeding specimens of humanity. Demon masks of ancient lacquer hung from the pillars, naked swords gleamed in motionless hands, and in a deep recess whose 'darkness' was rendered 'visible' by one lamp, was that indescribable horror the executioner of the Lord of Hell, his many brandished arms holding instruments of torture, and before him the bell, the thunderbolt and sceptre, the holy water, and the baptismal flagon. Our joss-sticks fumed on the still air, monks waved censers, and blasts of dissonant music woke the semi-subterranean echoes. In this temple of Justice the younger lamas spend some hours daily in the supposed contemplation of the torments reserved for the unholy. In the highest temple, that of Peace, the summer sunshine fell on Shakya Thubba and the Buddhist triad seated in endless serenity. The walls were covered with frescoes of great lamas, and a series of alcoves, each with an image representing an incarnation of Buddha, ran round

He who limps is still walking.
STANISLAW J. LEC

the temple. In a chapel full of monstrous images and piles of medallions made of the ashes of 'holy' men, the sub-abbot was discoursing to the acolytes on the religious classics. In the chapel of meditations, among lighted incense sticks, monks seated before images were telling their beads with the object of working themselves into a state of ecstatic contemplation (somewhat resembling a certain hypnotic trance), for there are undoubtedly devout Zaraas, though the majority are idle and unholy. It must be understood that all Tibetan literature is 'sacred' though some of the volumes of exquisite calligraphy on parchment, which for our benefit were divested of their silken and brocaded wrappings, contain nothing better than fairy tales and stories of doubtful morality, which are recited by the lamas to the accompaniment of incessant cups of chang, as a religious duty when they visit their 'flocks' in the winter.

The Deskyid gonpo contains 150 lamas, all of whom have been educated at Lhassa. A younger son in every household becomes a monk, and occasionally enters upon his vocation as an acolyte pupil as soon as weaned. At the age of thirteen these acolytes are sent to study at Lhassa for five or seven years, their departure being made the occasion of a great village feast, with several days of religious observances. The close connection with Lhassa, especially in the case of the yellow lamas, gives Nubra Buddhism a singular interest. All the larger gonpos have their prototype in Lhassa, all ceremonial has originated in Lhassa, every instrument of worship has been consecrated in Lhassa, and every lama is educated in the learning only to be obtained at Lhassa. Buddhism is indeed the most salient feature of Nubra. There are gonpos everywhere, the roads are lined by miles of chortens, manis, and prayer-mills, and flags inscribed with sacred words in Sanskrit flutter from every roof. There are processions of red and yellow lamas; every act in trade, agriculture, and social life needs the sanction of sacerdotalism; whatever exists of wealth is in the gonpos, which also have a monopoly of learning, and 11,000 monks closely linked with the laity, yet ruling all affairs of life and death and beyond death, are all connected by education, tradition, and authority with Lhassa.

ASIA

And forget not that the earth delights to feel your bare feet and the winds long to play with your hair.
KHALIL GIBRAN

We remained long on the blazing roof of the highest tower of the gonpo, while good Mr. Redslob disputed with the abbot 'concerning the things pertaining. to the kingdom of God.' The monks standing round laughed sneeringly. They had shown a little interest, Mr. R. said, on his earlier visits. The abbot accepted a copy of the Gospel of St. John.

'St. Matthew,' he observed, 'is very laughable reading.'

(From *Among the Tibetans*; Revell, New York, 1894)

Encounter with a Bear, 2007

DERVLA MURPHY

Septuagenarian Dervla Murphy travels from Moscow to the Russian Far East in the depths of winter. She seeks some time to herself staying beside Lake Baikal but is not alone on a walk through the snow.

For all his limited English, Fyodor perfectly understood my yearning to be more alone with Baikal than is possible in Ust-Barguzin. Looking conspiratorial, he revealed the existence of an isolated hunters' hut some six miles up the shore where I could commune with Lake Baikal in solitude. But he didn't want to be involved; the authorities might disapprove of a non-hunter, a foreign babushka, using this hut. It had a wood-stove and a supply of logs which hunters replenished before they left; leaving roubles instead would be OK. But could I cope with a wood-stove? Yes, nothing else heats my home. Candles would be needed – did I know about being very careful when using candles in a wooden hut? I assured Fyodor that I knew all about candles, had in the 1960s written two books by candlelight on a tiny island off the west coast of Ireland. He then sketched a map: I couldn't get lost, a little-used loggers' track led to the hut. But I mustn't go wandering off on vague inland paths through the taiga... I promised to keep close to the shore and decided to enjoy two reclusive nights; according to the weather forecast, there would be no 'winter-road' traffic before the weekend. 'If you start early,' said Fyodor, 'no one sees which way you turn.'

My God is the God of Walkers. If you walk hard enough, you probably don't need any other god. BRUCE CHATWIN

The hut track began not far from the Ski Lodge and I was on my way by dawn at – 21°c under a clear sky. The first climb was steep – and suddenly the taiga seemed hung with golden lanterns as the rising sun burnished each pine's frozen burden. On the ridge-top I hesitated and without Fyodor's sketch map would certainly have gone astray – straight ahead instead of sharp right. For a mile or so the lorry-wide track ran level on this long ridge: easy enough walking despite deepish snow. The stillness was absolute: not a bird fluttering. not a pine cone falling, no sound but my own squeaky-crunchy footsteps – until someone coughed hoarsely. I paused, slightly startled: no other prints marked the track's virgin snow. Looking towards the sound, I saw amidst the trees, scarcely twenty yards away, a large dark brown bear lumbering through snow almost up to his belly. Simultaneously the bear saw me and also paused, perhaps to consider this unexpected source of protein after his winter fast. Sensible Baikal bears hibernate until at least the end of March (I had checked with Fyodor) but perhaps the previous snowy day's warm noon hours – up to -13°c – had misled this one. Siberian bears like their meat and are six to seven feet tall when upright, a posture occasionally adopted to kill reindeer or people. As this fine specimen of *Ursus arctos* stood staring at me, most probably with no ill intent. I felt seriously frightened. Vividly I recalled advice given me forty years ago about the Himalayan black bear, also occasionally homicidal and sometimes encountered in those days (but probably not now) on mountain paths high above Dharamsala. 'Lie with your face to the ground. feigning dead. Don't try to run away, you'll lose the race. Bears like to amble but can move fast when they choose.' Snow had drifted to the side of the track between the bear and me and when I dropped out of his sight and lay flat I could hear my heart thumping with terror. It sounded louder then a gradually receding rustling crunch as the 'Master of the Taiga' went on his way. He was coughing again – could a chest infection have roused him prematurely? Reassuringly, his way was not my way; an hour later I saw his prints crossing the track.

(From *Silverland – A Winter Journey Beyond the Urals*; John Murray, London, 2007, © Dervla Murphy)

4

NORTH AMERICA

The Art of Walking, 1851
HENRY DAVID THOREAU

Henry David Thoreau (1817-62) was a keen advocate of walking and gave a lecture on the subject on April 23, 1851 at the Concord Lyceum. He gave this lecture several times during his life, building on his ideas, and the speech was published posthumously in the magazine Atlantic Monthly in 1862.

I have met with but one or two persons in the course of my life who understood the art of Walking, that is, of taking walks – who had a genius, so to speak, for SAUNTERING, which word is beautifully derived 'from idle people who roved about the country, in the Middle Ages, and asked charity, under pretense of going a la Sainte Terre,' to the Holy Land, till the children exclaimed, 'There goes à Sainte-Terrer,' a Saunterer, a Holy-Lander. They who never go to the Holy Land in their walks, as they pretend, are indeed mere idlers and vagabonds; but they who do go there are saunterers in the good sense, such as I mean. Some, however, would derive the word from *sans terre* without land or a home, which, therefore, in the good sense, will mean, having no particular home, but equally at home everywhere. For this is the secret of successful sauntering. He who sits still in a house all the time may be the greatest vagrant of all; but the saunterer, in the good sense, is no more vagrant than the meandering river, which is all the while sedulously seeking the shortest course to the sea. But I prefer the first, which, indeed, is the most probable derivation. For every walk is a sort of crusade, preached by some Peter the Hermit in us, to go forth and reconquer this Holy Land from the hands of the Infidels.

It is true, we are but faint-hearted crusaders, even the walkers, nowadays, who undertake no persevering, never-ending enterprises. Our expeditions are but tours, and come round again at evening to the old hearth-side from which we set out. Half the walk is but retracing our steps. We should go forth on the shortest walk, perchance, in the spirit of undying adventure, never to return – prepared to send back our embalmed hearts only as relics to our desolate kingdoms. If you are ready to leave father and mother, and brother and sister, and wife and child and friends, and never see them again – if you have paid your debts, and made your will, and settled all your affairs, and are a free man – then you are ready for a walk.

To come down to my own experience, my companion and I, for I sometimes have a companion, take pleasure in fancying ourselves knights of a new, or rather an old, order – not Equestrians or Chevaliers, not Ritters or Riders, but Walkers, a still more ancient and honorable class, I trust. The Chivalric and heroic spirit which once belonged to the Rider seems now to reside in, or perchance to have subsided into, the Walker – not the Knight, but Walker, Errant. He is a sort of fourth estate, outside of Church and State and People.

We have felt that we almost alone hereabouts practiced this noble art; though, to tell the truth, at least if their own assertions are to be received, most of my townsmen would fain walk sometimes, as I do, but they cannot. No wealth can buy the requisite leisure, freedom, and independence which are the capital in this profession. It comes only by the grace of God. It requires a direct dispensation from Heaven to become a walker. You must be born into the family of the Walkers. *Ambulator nascitur, non fit.*

☆　☆　☆

I think that I cannot preserve my health and spirits, unless I spend four hours a day at least – and it is commonly more than that – sauntering through the woods and over the hills and fields, absolutely free from all worldly engagements. You may safely say, A penny for your thoughts, or a thousand pounds. When sometimes I am reminded that the mechanics and shopkeepers stay in their shops not only all the forenoon, but all the afternoon too, sitting with crossed legs, so many of them – as if the legs were made to sit upon, and not to stand or walk upon – I think

It's Niagara Falls. It's one of the most beautiful natural wonders in the world. Who wouldn't want to walk across it?
NIK WALLENDA (TIGHTROPE WALKER)

that they deserve some credit for not having all committed suicide long ago.

I, who cannot stay in my chamber for a single day without acquiring some rust, and when sometimes I have stolen forth for a walk at the eleventh hour, or four o'clock in the afternoon, too late to redeem the day, when the shades of night were already beginning to be mingled with the daylight, have felt as if I had committed some sin to be atoned for, – I confess that I am astonished at the power of endurance, to say nothing of the moral insensibility, of my neighbors who confine themselves to shops and offices the whole day for weeks and months, aye, and years almost together. I know not what manner of stuff they are of – sitting there now at three o'clock in the afternoon, as if it were three o'clock in the morning. Bonaparte may talk of the three-o'clock-in-the-morning courage, but it is nothing to the courage which can sit down cheerfully at this hour in the afternoon over against one's self whom you have known all the morning, to starve out a garrison to whom you are bound by such strong ties of sympathy. I wonder that about this time, or say between four and five o'clock in the afternoon, too late for the morning papers and too early for the evening ones, there is not a general explosion heard up and down the street, scattering a legion of antiquated and house-bred notions and whims to the four winds for an airing – and so the evil cure itself.

How womankind, who are confined to the house still more than men, stand it I do not know; but I have ground to suspect that most of them do not STAND it at all. When, early in a summer afternoon, we have been shaking the dust of the village from the skirts of our garments, making haste past those houses with purely Doric or Gothic fronts, which have such an air of repose about them, my companion whispers that probably about these times their occupants are all gone to bed. Then it is that I appreciate the beauty and the glory of architecture, which itself never turns in, but forever stands out and erect, keeping watch over the slumberers.

No doubt temperament, and, above all, age, have a good deal to do with it. As a man grows older, his ability to sit still and follow indoor occupations increases. He grows vespertinal in his habits as the evening of life approaches, till at last he comes forth only just before sundown, and gets all the walk that he requires in half an hour.

But the walking of which I speak has nothing in it akin to taking exercise, as it is called, as the sick take medicine at stated hours – as the Swinging of dumb-bells or chairs; but is itself the enterprise and adventure of the day. If you would get exercise, go in search of the springs of life. Think of a man's swinging dumb-bells for his health, when those springs are bubbling up in far-off pastures unsought by him!

Moreover, you must walk like a camel, which is said to be the only beast which ruminates when walking. When a traveler asked Wordsworth's servant to show him her master's study, she answered, 'Here is his library, but his study is out of doors.'

(From *Walking*, published in *Atlantic Monthly*, Boston, 1862)

Climbing in the Rockies, 1873

ISABELLA BIRD

Isabella Bird (1831-1904) was the Dervla Murphy of the 19th century: a tremendously intrepid travel writer and photographer who continued her travels until well into old age. She visited many parts of the world at a time when simply getting there was a hard journey in itself and her books were very popular. On one trip she travelled more than 800 miles through the Rockies on horseback, part of the time in the company of a rough outlaw known as 'Rocky Mountain Jim' and his faithful dog, Ring. To reach the top of Long's Peak she has to get off the horse and climb.

Long's Peak, 'the American Matterhorn,' as some call it, was ascended five years ago for the first time. I thought I should like to attempt it, but up to Monday, when Evans left for Denver, cold water was thrown upon the project. It was too late in the season, the winds were likely to be strong, etc.; but just before leaving, Evans said that the weather was looking more settled, and if I did not get farther than the timber line it would be worth going. Soon

I walk slowly, but I never walk backward.
ABRAHAM LINCOLN

after he left, 'Mountain Jim' came in, and said he would go up as guide, and the two youths who rode here with me from Longmount and I caught at the proposal. Mrs. Edwards at once baked bread for three days, steaks were cut from the steer which hangs up conveniently, and tea, sugar, and butter were benevolently added. Our picnic was not to be a luxurious or 'well-found' one, for, in order to avoid the expense of a pack mule, we limited our luggage to what our saddle horses could carry. Behind my saddle I carried three pair of camping blankets and a quilt, which reached to my shoulders. My own boots were so much worn that it was painful to walk, even about the park, in them, so Evans had lent me a pair of his hunting boots, which hung to the horn of my saddle. The horses of the two young men were equally loaded, for we had to prepare for many degrees of frost. Jim was a shocking figure; he had on an old pair of high boots, with a baggy pair of old trousers made of deer hide, held on by an old scarf tucked into them; a leather shirt, with three or four ragged unbuttoned waistcoats over it; an old smashed wideawake, from under which his tawny, neglected ringlets hung; and with his one eye, his one long spur, his knife in his belt, his revolver in his waistcoat pocket, his saddle covered with an old beaver skin, from which the paws hung down; his camping blankets behind him, his rifle laid across the saddle in front of him, and his axe, canteen, and other gear hanging to the horn, he was as awful-looking a ruffian as one could see. By way of contrast he rode a small Arab mare, of exquisite beauty, skittish, high spirited, gentle, but altogether too light for him, and he fretted her incessantly to make her display herself.

From the dry, buff grass of Estes Park we turned off up a trail on the side of a pine-hung gorge, up a steep pine-clothed hill, down to a small valley, rich in fine, sun-cured hay about eighteen inches high, and enclosed by high mountains whose deepest hollow contains a lily-covered lake, fitly named 'The Lake of the Lilies.' Ah, how magical its beauty was, as it slept in silence, while THERE the dark pines were mirrored motionless in its pale gold, and HERE the great white lily cups and dark green leaves rested on amethyst-colored water!

The pay is good and I can walk to work.
JOHN F. KENNEDY

From this we ascended into the purple gloom of great pine forests which clothe the skirts of the mountains up to a height of about 11,000 feet, and from their chill and solitary depths we had glimpses of golden atmosphere and rose-lit summits, not of 'the land very far off,' but of the land nearer now in all its grandeur, gaining in sublimity by nearness – glimpses, too, through a broken vista of purple gorges, of the illimitable Plains lying idealized in the late sunlight, their baked, brown expanse transfigured into the likeness of a sunset sea rolling infinitely in waves of misty gold.

☆　☆　☆

The timber line was passed, but yet a little higher a slope of mountain meadow dipped to the south-west towards a bright stream trickling under ice and icicles, and there a grove of the beautiful silver spruce marked our camping ground. The trees were in miniature, but so exquisitely arranged that one might well ask what artist's hand had planted them, scattering them here, clumping them there, and training their slim spires towards heaven. Hereafter, when I call up memories of the glorious, the view from this camping ground will come up. Looking east, gorges opened to the distant Plains, then fading into purple grey. Mountains with pine-clothed skirts rose in ranges, or, solitary, uplifted their grey summits, while close behind, but nearly 3,000 feet above us, towered the bald white crest of Long's Peak, its huge precipices red with the light of a sun long lost to our eyes.

☆　☆　☆

Unsaddling and picketing the horses securely, making the beds of pine shoots, and dragging up logs for fuel, warmed us all. Jim built up a great fire, and before long we were all sitting around it at supper. It didn't matter much that we had to drink our tea out of the battered meat tins in which it was boiled, and eat strips of beef reeking with pine smoke without plates or forks. 'Treat Jim as a gentleman and you'll find him one,' I had been told; and though his manner was certainly bolder and freer than that of gentlemen generally, no imaginary fault could be found. He was very agreeable as a man of culture as well as a child of

The lack of power to take joy in outdoor nature is as real a misfortune as the lack of power to take joy in books.
THEODORE ROOSEVELT

nature; the desperado was altogether out of sight. He was very courteous and even kind to me, which was fortunate, as the young men had little idea of showing even ordinary civilities. That night I made the acquaintance of his dog Ring, said to be the best hunting dog in Colorado, with the body and legs of a collie, but a head approaching that of a mastiff, a noble face with a wistful human expression, and the most truthful eyes I ever saw in an animal. His master loves him if he loves anything, but in his savage moods ill-treats him. Ring's devotion never swerves, and his truthful eyes are rarely taken off his master's face. He is almost human in his intelligence, and, unless he is told to do so, he never takes notice of any one but 'Jim.' In a tone as if speaking to a human being, his master, pointing to me, said, 'Ring, go to that lady, and don't leave her again to-night.' Ring at once came to me, looked into my face, laid his head on my shoulder, and then lay down beside me with his head on my lap, but never taking his eyes from Jim's face.

The long shadows of the pines lay upon the frosted grass, an aurora leaped fitfully, and the moonlight, though intensely bright, was pale beside the red, leaping flames of our pine logs and their red glow on our gear, ourselves, and Ring's truthful face. One of the young men sang a Latin student's song and two Negro melodies; the other 'Sweet Spirit, hear my Prayer.' Jim sang one of Moore's melodies in a singular falsetto, and all together sang, 'The Star-spangled Banner' and 'The Red, White, and Blue.' Then Jim recited a very clever poem of his own composition, and told some fearful Indian stories. A group of small silver spruces away from the fire was my sleeping place. The artist who had been up there had so woven and interlaced their lower branches as to form a bower, affording at once shelter from the wind and a most agreeable privacy. It was thickly strewn with young pine shoots, and these, when covered with a blanket, with an inverted saddle for a pillow, made a luxurious bed. The mercury at 9 p.m. was 12 degrees below the freezing point. Jim, after a last look at the horses, made a huge fire, and stretched himself out beside it, but Ring lay at my back to keep me warm. I could not sleep, but the night passed rapidly. I was

A dog is one of the remaining reasons why some people can be persuaded to go for a walk.
O.A. BATTISTA

anxious about the ascent, for gusts of ominous sound swept through the pines at intervals. Then wild animals howled, and Ring was perturbed in spirit about them. Then it was strange to see the notorious desperado, a red-handed man, sleeping as quietly as innocence sleeps. But, above all, it was exciting to lie there, with no better shelter than a bower of pines, on a mountain 11,000 feet high, in the very heart of the Rocky Range, under twelve degrees of frost, hearing sounds of wolves, with shivering stars looking through the fragrant canopy, with arrowy pines for bed-posts, and for a night lamp the red flames of a camp-fire.

☆ ☆ ☆

Jim had advised me against taking any wraps, and my thin Hawaiian riding dress, only fit for the tropics, was penetrated by the keen air. The rarefied atmosphere soon began to oppress our breathing, and I found that Evans's boots were so large that I had no foothold. Fortunately, before the real difficulty of the ascent began, we found, under a rock, a pair of small overshoes, probably left by the Hayden exploring expedition, which just lasted for the day. As we were leaping from rock to rock, Jim said, 'I was thinking in the night about your traveling alone, and wondering where you carried your Derringer, for I could see no signs of it.' On my telling him that I traveled unarmed, he could hardly believe it, and adjured me to get a revolver at once.

☆ ☆ ☆

You know I have no head and no ankles, and never ought to dream of mountaineering; and had I known that the ascent was a real mountaineering feat I should not have felt the slightest ambition to perform it. As it is, I am only humiliated by my success, for Jim dragged me up, like a bale of goods, by sheer force of muscle. At the 'Notch' the real business of the ascent began. Two thousand feet of solid rock towered above us, four thousand feet of broken rock shelved precipitously below; smooth granite ribs, with barely a foothold, stood out here and there; melted snow refrozen several times, presented a more serious obstacle; many of the rocks were loose, and tumbled down when touched. To me

Man's heart away from nature becomes hard.
STANDING BEAR

it was a time of extreme terror. I was roped to Jim, but it was of no use; my feet were paralyzed and slipped on the bare rock, and he said it was useless to try to go that way, and we retraced our steps. I wanted to return to the 'Notch,' knowing that my incompetence would detain the party, and one of the young men said almost plainly that a woman was a dangerous encumbrance, but the trapper replied shortly that if it were not to take a lady up he would not go up at all. He went on to explore, and reported that further progress on the correct line of ascent was blocked by ice; and then for two hours we descended, lowering ourselves by our hands from rock to rock along a boulder-strewn sweep of 4,000 feet, patched with ice and snow, and perilous from rolling stones. My fatigue, giddiness, and pain from bruised ankles, and arms half pulled out of their sockets, were so great that I should never have gone halfway had not Jim, nolens volens, dragged me along with a patience and skill, and withal a determination that I should ascend the Peak, which never failed. After descending about 2,000 feet to avoid the ice, we got into a deep ravine with inaccessible sides, partly filled with ice and snow and partly with large and small fragments of rock, which were constantly giving away, rendering the footing very insecure. That part to me was two hours of painful and unwilling submission to the inevitable; of trembling, slipping, straining, of smooth ice appearing when it was least expected, and of weak entreaties to be left behind while the others went on. Jim always said that there was no danger, that there was only a short bad bit ahead, and that I should go up even if he carried me!

Slipping, faltering, gasping from the exhausting toil in the rarefied air, with throbbing hearts and panting lungs, we reached the top of the gorge and squeezed ourselves between two gigantic fragments of rock by a passage called the 'Dog's Lift,' when I climbed on the shoulders of one man and then was hauled up. This introduced us by an abrupt turn round the south-west angle of the Peak to a narrow shelf of considerable length, rugged, uneven, and so overhung by the cliff in some places that it is necessary to crouch to pass at all. Above, the Peak looks nearly vertical for 400 feet; and below, the most tremendous precipice I

If one morning I walked on top of the water across the Potomac River, the headline that afternoon would read: 'President Can't Swim.' LYNDON B. JOHNSON

have ever seen descends in one unbroken fall. This is usually considered the most dangerous part of the ascent, but it does not seem so to me, for such foothold as there is is secure, and one fancies that it is possible to hold on with the hands. But there, and on the final, and, to my thinking, the worst part of the climb, one slip, and a breathing, thinking, human being would lie 3,000 feet below, a shapeless, bloody heap! Ring refused to traverse the Ledge, and remained at the 'Lift' howling piteously.

From thence the view is more magnificent even than that from the 'Notch.' At the foot of the precipice below us lay a lovely lake, wood embosomed, from or near which the bright St. Vrain and other streams take their rise. I thought how their clear cold waters, growing turbid in the affluent flats, would heat under the tropic sun, and eventually form part of that great ocean river which renders our far-off islands habitable by impinging on their shores. Snowy ranges, one behind the other, extended to the distant horizon, folding in their wintry embrace the beauties of Middle Park. Pike's Peak, more than one hundred miles off, lifted that vast but shapeless summit which is the landmark of southern Colorado. There were snow patches, snow slashes, snow abysses, snow forlorn and soiled looking, snow pure and dazzling, snow glistening above the purple robe of pine worn by all the mountains; while away to the east, in limitless breadth, stretched the green-grey of the endless Plains. Giants everywhere reared their splintered crests. From thence, with a single sweep, the eye takes in a distance of 300 miles – that distance to the west, north, and south being made up of mountains ten, eleven, twelve, and thirteen thousand feet in height, dominated by Long's Peak, Gray's Peak, and Pike's Peak, all nearly the height of Mont Blanc! On the Plains we traced the rivers by their fringe of cottonwoods to the distant Platte, and between us and them lay glories of mountain, canyon, and lake, sleeping in depths of blue and purple most ravishing to the eye.

As we crept from the ledge round a horn of rock I beheld what made me perfectly sick and dizzy to look at – the terminal Peak itself – a smooth, cracked face or wall of pink granite, as nearly perpendicular as anything could well be up which it was possible to climb, well deserving the name of the 'American Matterhorn.'

Scaling, not climbing, is the correct term for this last ascent. It took one hour to accomplish 500 feet, pausing for breath every minute or two. The only foothold was in narrow cracks or on minute projections on the granite. To get a toe in these cracks, or here and there on a scarcely obvious projection, while crawling on hands and knees, all the while tortured with thirst and gasping and struggling for breath, this was the climb; but at last the Peak was won. A grand, well-defined mountain top it is, a nearly level acre of boulders, with precipitous sides all round, the one we came up being the only accessible one.

It was not possible to remain long. One of the young men was seriously alarmed by bleeding from the lungs, and the intense dryness of the day and the rarefication of the air, at a height of nearly 15,000 feet, made respiration very painful. There is always water on the Peak, but it was frozen as hard as a rock, and the sucking of ice and snow increases thirst. We all suffered severely from the want of water, and the gasping for breath made our mouths and tongues so dry that articulation was difficult, and the speech of all unnatural.

From the summit were seen in unrivalled combination all the views which had rejoiced our eyes during the ascent. It was something at last to stand upon the storm-rent crown of this lonely sentinel of the Rocky Range, on one of the mightiest of the vertebrae of the backbone of the North American continent, and to see the waters start for both oceans.

(From *A Lady's Life in the Rocky Mountains*; GP Putnam's Sons, 1886)

Up-hill, 1861

CHRISTINA ROSSETTI

In some of the poems of Christina Rossetti (1830-94), it is the very simplicity that evokes the profound meaning in the piece.

Does the road wind up-hill all the way?
   Yes, to the very end.

**Falling leaves
hide the path
so quietly.** JOHN BAILEY, *AUTUMN HAIKU*

Will the day's journey take the whole long day?
  From morn to night, my friend.

But is there for the night a resting-place?
  A roof for when the slow dark hours begin.
May not the darkness hide it from my face?
  You cannot miss that inn.

Shall I meet other wayfarers at night?
  Those who have gone before.
Then must I knock, or call when just in sight?
  They will not keep you standing at that door.

Shall I find comfort, travel-sore and weak?
  Of labour you shall find the sum.
Will there be beds for me and all who seek?
  Yea, beds for all who come.

(From *Macmillan's Magazine*, February 1861)

Sunset, 1862
HENRY DAVID THOREAU

*Henry David Thoreau (1817-62) studied at Harvard and was a philoso-
pher, poet and naturalist. He was keen on a life outdoors and said: 'Most
of the luxuries and many of the so-called comforts of life are not only not
indispensable, but positive hindrances to the elevation of mankind'. He
was interested in Indian thought and customs and his philosophy of
civil disobedience is said to have influenced Mahatma Gandhi (see p94).*

Every sunset which I witness inspires me with the desire to go to
a West as distant and as fair as that into which the sun goes
down. He appears to migrate westward daily, and tempt us to
follow him. He is the Great Western Pioneer whom the nations
follow. We dream all night of those mountain-ridges in the horizon, though they may be of vapor only, which were last gilded by
his rays. The island of Atlantis, and the islands and gardens of the
Hesperides, a sort of terrestrial paradise, appear to have been the

Keep close to Nature's heart ... and break clear away, once
in awhile, and climb a mountain or spend a week in the
woods. Wash your spirit clean. JOHN MUIR

Great West of the ancients, enveloped in mystery and poetry. Who has not seen in imagination, when looking into the sunset sky, the gardens of the Hesperides, and the foundation of all those fables?

☆ ☆ ☆

We had a remarkable sunset one day last November. I was walking in a meadow, the source of a small brook, when the sun at last, just before setting, after a cold, gray day, reached a clear stratum in the horizon, and the softest, brightest morning sunlight fell on the dry grass and on the stems of the trees in the opposite horizon and on the leaves of the shrub oaks on the hillside, while our shadows stretched long over the meadow eastward, as if we were the only motes in its beams. It was such a light as we could not have imagined a moment before, and the air also was so warm and serene that nothing was wanting to make a paradise of that meadow. When we reflected that this was not a solitary phenomenon, never to happen again, but that it would happen forever and ever, an infinite number of evenings, and cheer and reassure the latest child that walked there, it was more glorious still.

The sun sets on some retired meadow, where no house is visible, with all the glory and splendor that it lavishes on cities, and perchance as it has never set before – where there is but a solitary marsh hawk to have his wings gilded by it, or only a musquash looks out from his cabin, and there is some little black-veined brook in the midst of the marsh, just beginning to meander, winding slowly round a decaying stump. We walked in so pure and bright a light, gilding the withered grass and leaves, so softly and serenely bright, I thought I had never bathed in such a golden flood, without a ripple or a murmur to it. The west side of every wood and rising ground gleamed like the boundary of Elysium, and the sun on our backs seemed like a gentle herdsman driving us home at evening.

(From *Walking*, published in *Atlantic Monthly*, Boston, 1862)

An early-morning walk is a blessing for the whole day. H.D. THOREAU

SOUTH AMERICA

5

First impressions of Brazil, 1848
HENRY WALTER BATES

Henry Walter Bates (1825-92) was a distinguished naturalist who during trips to the Amazon beginning in 1848 collected almost 15,000 specimens, more than half of which had never before been recorded.

I embarked at Liverpool, with Mr. Wallace, in a small trading vessel, on the 26th of April, 1848; and, after a swift passage from the Irish Channel to the equator, arrived, on the 26th of May, off Salinas. This is the pilot-station for vessels bound to Pará, the only port of entry to the vast region watered by the Amazons. It is a small village, formerly a missionary settlement of the Jesuits, situated a few miles to the eastward of the Pará River.

Here the ship anchored in the open sea at a distance of six miles from the shore, the shallowness of the water far out around the mouth of the great river not permitting, in safety, a nearer approach; and, the signal was hoisted for a pilot.

It was with deep interest that my companion and myself, both now about to see and examine the beauties of a tropical country for the first time, gazed on the land where I, at least, eventually spent eleven of the best years of my life. To the eastward the country was not remarkable in appearance, being slightly undulating, with bare sand-hills and scattered trees; but to the west-ward, stretching towards the mouth of the river, we could see through the captain's glass a long line of for-est, rising apparently out of the water; a densely-packed mass of tall trees, broken into groups, and finally into single trees, as it dwindled away in the distance. This was the frontier, in this direction, of the great primaeval forest characteristic of this region, which contains so many wonders in its recesses, and clothes the whole surface of the country for two thousand miles from this point to the foot of the Andes.

☆   ☆   ☆

We went ashore in due time, and were kindly received by Mr. Miller, the consignee of the vessel, who invited us to make his house our home until we could obtain a suitable residence. On landing, the hot moist mouldy air, which seemed to strike from the ground and walls, reminded me of the atmosphere of tropical stoves at Kew. In the course of the afternoon a heavy shower fell, and in the evening, the atmosphere having been cooled by the rain, we walked about a mile out of town to the residence of an American gentleman to whom our host wished to introduce us.

The impressions received during this first walk can never wholly fade from my mind. After traversing the few streets of tall, gloomy, convent-looking buildings near the port, inhabited chiefly by merchants and shopkeepers, along which idle soldiers, dressed in shabby uniforms carrying their muskets carelessly over their arms, priests, negresses with red water-jars on their heads, sad-looking Indian women carrying their naked children astride on their hips, and other samples of the motley life of the place, we passed down a long narrow street leading to the suburbs. Beyond this, our road lay across a grassy common into a picturesque lane leading to the virgin forest. The long street was inhabited by the poorer class of the population. The houses were of one story only, and had an irregular and mean appearance. The windows were without glass, having, instead, projecting lattice casements. The street was unpaved, and inches deep in loose sand. Groups of people were cooling themselves outside their doors – people of all shades in colour of skin, European, Negro and Indian, but chiefly an uncertain mixture of the three. Amongst them were several handsome women dressed in a slovenly manner, barefoot or shod in loose slippers, but wearing richly-decorated earrings, and around their necks strings of very large gold beads. They had dark expressive eyes, and remarkably rich heads of hair. It was a mere fancy, but I thought the mingled squalor, luxuriance and beauty of these women were pointedly in

No city should be too large for a man to walk out of in a morning. CYRIL CONNOLLY harmony with the rest of the scene – so striking, in the view, was the mixture of natural riches and human poverty. The houses were mostly in a dilapidated condition, and signs of indolence and neglect were visible everywhere. The wooden palings which surrounded the weed-grown gardens were strewn about and broken; hogs, goats, and ill-fed poultry wandered in and out through the gaps. But amidst all, and compensating every defect, rose the overpowering beauty of the vegetation. The massive dark crowns of shady mangos were seen everywhere amongst the dwellings, amidst fragrant blossoming orange, lemon, and many other tropical fruit trees, some in flower, others in fruit, at varying stages of ripeness. Here and there, shooting above the more dome-like and sombre trees, were the smooth columnar stems of palms, bearing aloft their magnificent crowns of finely-cut fronds. Amongst the latter the slim assai-palm was especially noticeable, growing in groups of four or five; its smooth, gently-curving stem, twenty to thirty feet high, terminating in a head of feathery foliage, inexpressibly light and elegant in outline. On the boughs of the taller and more ordinary-looking trees sat tufts of curiously-leaved parasites. Slender, woody lianas hung in festoons from the branches, or were suspended in the form of cords and ribbons; whilst luxuriant creeping plants overran alike tree-trunks, roofs and walls, or toppled over palings in a copious profusion of foliage.

The superb banana (*Musa paradisiaca*), of which I had always read as forming one of the charms of tropical vegetation, grew here with great luxuriance – its glossy velvety-green leaves, twelve feet in length, curving over the roofs of verandahs in the rear of every house. The shape of the leaves, the varying shades of green which they present when lightly moved by the wind, and especially the contrast they afford in colour and form to the more sombre hues and more rounded outline of the other trees, are quite sufficient to account for the charm of this glorious tree.

Strange forms of vegetation drew our attention at almost every step. Amongst them were the different kinds of Bromelia, or pine-apple plants, with their long, rigid, sword-shaped leaves, in some species jagged or toothed along their edges. Then there

SOUTH AMERICA

was the bread-fruit tree – an importation, it is true; but remarkable from its large, glossy, dark green, strongly digitated foliage, and its interesting history. Many other trees and plants, curious in leaf, stem, or manner of growth, grew on the borders of the thickets along which lay our road; they were all attractive to newcomers, whose last country ramble of quite recent date was over the bleak moors of Derbyshire on a sleety morning in April.

As we continued our walk the brief twilight commenced, and the sounds of multifarious life came from the vegetation around. The whirring of cicadas; the shrill stridulation of a vast number and variety of field crickets and grasshoppers, each species sounding its peculiar note; the plaintive hooting of tree frogs – all blended together in one continuous ringing sound – the audible expression of the teeming profusion of Nature. As night came on, many species of frogs and toads in the marshy places joined in the chorus – their croaking and drumming, far louder than anything I had before heard in the same line, being added to the other noises, created an almost deafening din. This uproar of life, I afterwards found, never wholly ceased, night or day. In the course of time I became, like other residents, accustomed to it. It is, however, one of the peculiarities of a tropical – at least, a Brazilian – climate which is most likely to surprise a stranger. After my return to England, the deathlike stillness of summer days in the country appeared to me as strange as the ringing uproar did on my first arrival at Pará.

(From *The Naturalist on the River Amazons;* John Murray, London, 1863)

It seems very safe to me to be surrounded by green growing things and water.
BARBARA KINGSOLVER

SOUTH AMERICA

The Ritual of My Legs, 1931

Pablo Neruda

In the final verses of his poem, Pablo Neruda (1904-73) reflects on his sense of separateness between his body and the world

From the knee to the foot a hard form,
mineral, coldly useful, appears,
a creature of bone and persistence,
and the ankles are now nothing but the naked purpose,
exactitude and necessity definitively exposed.

Without sensuality, short and hard, and masculine,
my legs exist, there, and endowed
with muscular groups like complementary animals,
and there too a life, a solid, subtle, sharp life
endures without trembling, waiting and performing.

At my feet ticklish
and hard like the sun, and open like flowers,
and perpetual, magnificent soldiers
in the grey war of space
everything ends, life definitively ends at my feet,
what is foreign and hostile begins there:
the names of the world, the frontier and the remote,
the substantive and the adjectival too great for my heart
originate there with dense and cold constancy.

Always,
manufactured products, socks, shoes,
or simply infinite air,
there will be between my feet and the earth
stressing the isolated and solitary part of my being,
something tenaciously involved between my life and the earth,
something openly unconquerable and unfriendly.

From *The Ritual of My Legs (Ritual de mis piernas)*; © Pablo Neruda, 1931)

SOUTH AMERICA

**I stroll along serenely, with my eyes, my shoes,
my rage, forgetting everything.**
Pablo Neruda

Mountain-sickness on Chimborazo, 1880
EDWARD WHYMPER

Edward Whymper (1840-1911) was an explorer and mountaineer, and is best known for making the first ascent of the Matterhorn in 1865. He travelled to Ecuador in 1880, with Italian guides Louis and Jean-Antoine Carrel, to study the effects of altitude sickness, known then as 'mountain-sickness'. As they climb Chimborazo, the condition finally strikes them...

Neither of the two Carrels, nor I myself, had ever experienced the least symptom of mountain-sickness. None of us, however, prior to this journey had been 16,000 feet high; and, probably, had never sustained so low a pressure as 17 inches. I had at various times been in the company of persons who said they were affected by 'rarefaction of the air,' and who were unable to proceed; but their symptoms, so far as I observed them, might have been produced by fatigue and unfamiliarity with mountaineering, and were not of the more acute kind. Although I attached little importance to such cases as had come under my own personal observation, I had never felt disposed to question the *reality* of mountain-sickness; and on the contrary had frequently maintained that it is reasonable to expect some effects should be produced upon men who experience much lower atmospheric pressures than those to which they are accustomed; and that it is much more remarkable to find that, *apparently*, no effects of a detrimental kind are caused on many persons who ascend to the height of 14-15,000 feet (or, say, sustain a pressure of seventeen and a half inches), than it is to learn that others have suffered at slightly lower pressures.

☆ ☆ ☆

[In the camp at 16,000ft] We were feverish, had intense headaches, and were unable to satisfy our desire for air, except by breathing with open mouths. This naturally parched the throat, and produced a craving for drink, which we were unable to satisfy, – partly from the difficulty in obtaining it, and partly from trouble in swallowing it. When we got enough, we could only sip, and not to save our lives could we have taken a quarter of a

Walking is also an ambulation of mind.
GRETEL EHRLICH

pint at a draught. Before a mouthful was down, we were obliged to breathe and gasp again, until our throats were as dry as ever. Besides having our normal rate of breathing largely accelerated, we found it impossible to sustain life without every now and then giving spasmodic gulps, just like fishes when taken out of water. Of course there was no inclination to eat ; but we wished to smoke, and found that our pipes almost refused to burn, for they, like ourselves, wanted more oxygen.

This condition of affairs lasted all night, and all the next day, and I then managed to pluck up spirit enough to get out some chlorate of potash, which by the advice of Dr. W. Marcet, had been brought in case of need. Chlorate of potash was, I believe, first used in mountain travel by Dr. Henderson, in the Karakorum range, and it was subsequently employed on Sir Douglas Forsyth's Mission to Yarkund in 1873-4, apparently with good effect ... The large proportion of oxygen contained in the salt probably supplies to the blood what in these regions it fails to derive from the air, and thus restores through the stomach what the lungs lose. Whatever the explanation of its action, however, there is no doubt of its efficacy in relieving the dreadful nausea and headache produced by the circulation of an inefficiently oxygenated blood.

☆　☆　☆

Louis Carrel also submitted himself to experiment, and seemed to derive benefit; but Jean-Antoine sturdily refused to take any 'doctor's stuff,' which he regarded as an insult to intelligence. For all human ills, for every complaint, from dysentery to want of air, there was, in his opinion, but one remedy; and that was Wine; most efficacious always if taken hot, more especially if a little spice and sugar were added to it.

The stories that he related respecting the virtues of Red wine would be enough to fill a book. The wine must be Red – 'White wine,' he used to say dogmatically, 'is bad, it cuts the legs.' Most of these legends I cannot remember, but there was one which it was impossible to forget, commencing thus. 'Red wine when heated and beaten up with raw eggs is good for many complaints – particularly at the Eve of St. John, when the moon is at

If you are seeking creative ideas, go out walking. Angels whisper to a man when he goes for a walk. RAYMOND INMON

the full, for women who are in the family way; provided it is drunk whilst looking over the left shoulder, and' – I never heard the end of that story, because I laughed too soon.

His opinions upon things in general were often very original, and I learned much whilst in his company; amongst the rest, that, for the cure of headache, nothing better can be mentioned than keeping the head warm and the feet cold. It is only fair to say that he practised what he preached. I can remember no more curious sight than that of this middle-aged man, lying nearly obscured under a pile of ponchos, with his head bound up in a wonderful arrangement of handkerchiefs, vainly attempting to smoke a short pipe whilst gasping like a choking cod-fish, his naked feet sticking out from underneath his blankets when the temperature in the tent was much below the freezing-point.

Strange to relate, Mr. Perring did not appear to be affected at all. Except for him we should have fared badly. He kept the fire going – no easy task, for the fire appeared to suffer from the want of air just like ourselves, and required such incessant blowing that I shall consider for the future a pair of bellows an indispensable item in a mountaineer's equipment. Mr. Perring behaved on this occasion in an exemplary manner. He melted snow, and brought us drink, and attended to our wants in general, and did not seem any worse at the second camp than at Guaranda. Yet he was a rather debilitated man, and was distinctly less robust than ourselves. He could scarcely walk on a flat road without desiring to sit down, or traverse a hundred yards on a mountain side without being obliged to rest. It is natural to enquire how can one account for this man of enfeebled constitution being unaffected, when three others, who were all more or less accustomed to high elevations (low pressures) were rendered, for a time, completely incapable?

(From Travels Amongst the Great Andes of the Equator;
John Murray, London, 1892)

I no longer want to walk on worn soles.
FRIEDRICH NIETZSCHE

The Diet of an Amazonian Entomologist, 1848
Henry Walter Bates

August 6th and 7th. – I was very successful at this place with regard to the objects of my journey. About twenty new species of fishes and a considerable number of small reptiles were added to my collection; but very few birds were met with worth preserving. A great number of the most conspicuous insects of the locality were new to me, and turned out to be species peculiar to this part of the Amazons valley.

The most interesting acquisition was a large and handsome monkey, of a species I had not before met with – the white-whiskered Coaitá, or spider-monkey (*Ateles marginatus*). I saw a pair one day in the forest moving slowly along the branches of a lofty tree, and shot one of them; the next day John Aracu brought down another, possibly the companion. The species is of about the same size as the common black kind, of which I have given an account in a former chapter, and has a similar lean body, with limbs clothed with coarse black hair; but it differs in having the whiskers and a triangular patch on the crown of the head of a white colour. I thought the meat the best flavoured I had ever tasted. It resembled beef, but had a richer and sweeter taste.

During the time of our stay in this part of the Cuparí, we could get scarcely anything but fish to eat, and as this diet disagreed with me, three successive days of it reducing me to a state of great weakness, I was obliged to make the most of our Coaitá meat. We smoke-dried the joints instead of salting them, placing them for several hours upon a framework of sticks arranged over a fire, a plan adopted by the natives to preserve fish when they have no salt, and which they call 'muquiar.' Meat putrefies in this climate in less than twenty-four hours, and salting is of no use, unless the pieces are cut in thin slices and dried immediately in the sun. My monkeys lasted me about a fortnight, the last joint being an arm with the clenched fist, which I used with great economy, hanging it in the intervals, between my frugal meals, on a nail in the cabin. Nothing but the hardest necessity could have driven me so near to

SOUTH AMERICA

cannibalism as this, but we had the greatest difficulty in obtaining here a sufficient supply of animal food. About every three days the work on the montaria had to be suspended, and all hands turned out for the day to hunt and fish, in which they were often unsuccessful, for although there was plenty of game in the forest, it was too widely scattered to be available. Ricardo, and Alberto occasionally brought in a tortoise or ant-eater, which served us for one day's consumption. We made acquaintance here with many strange dishes, amongst them Iguana eggs; these are of oblong form, about an inch in length, and covered with a flexible shell. The lizard lays about two score of them in the hollows of trees. They have an oily taste; the men ate them raw, beaten up with farinha, mixing a pinch of salt in the mess; I could only do with them when mixed with Tucupí sauce, of which we had a large jar full always ready to temper unsavoury morsels.

One day as I was entomologising alone and unarmed, in a dry Ygapó, where the trees were rather wide apart and the ground coated to the depth of eight or ten inches with dead leaves, I was near coming into collision with a boa constrictor. I had just entered a little thicket to capture an insect, and whilst pinning it was rather startled by a rushing noise in the vicinity. I looked up to the sky, thinking a squall was coming on, but not a breath of wind stirred in the tree-tops. On stepping out of the bushes I met face to face a huge serpent coming down a slope, making the dry twigs crack and fly with his weight as he moved over them. I had very frequently met with a smaller boa, the Cutimboia, in a similar way, and knew from the habits of the family that there was no danger, so I stood my ground. On seeing me the reptile suddenly turned and glided at an accelerated pace down the path. Wishing to take a note of his probable size and the colours and markings of his skin, I set off after him; but he increased his speed, and I was unable to get near enough for the purpose. There was very little of the serpentine movement in his course. The rapidly moving and shining body looked like a stream of brown liquid flowing over the thick bed of fallen leaves, rather than a serpent with skin of varied colours.

(From *The Naturalist on the River Amazons*; John Murray, London, 1863)

I have the European urge to use my feet when a drive can be dispensed with.
VLADIMIR NABOKOV, *LOLITA*

AFRICA

6

Searching for Crayfish, 1905
ARTHUR E.P. WEIGALL

Arthur Weigall (1880-1934) began his working life as an Egyptologist working with Flinders Petrie and Howard Carter but after his marriage to pianist Muriel Lillie he became a set designer and lyricist for revues and plays on the London stage. Travelling by the Red Sea he visits Kossair, once on the trade route to India, but now a 'sleepy town ... of lotos-eaters... There is very little to be done here, and most of the inhabitants sleep for two-thirds of the day'. He persuades some fisherman to take him out over the reach to look for crayfish.

In camp the remainder of the day was spent in that vague pottering which the presence of the sea always induces. There were some beautiful shells upon the shore to attract one, and natives brought others for sale, lying down to sleep in the shade of the kitchen tent until we deigned to give them attention. There were sketches to be made and photographs to be taken. Amidst the houses at the south end of the town some fragments of a Ptolemaic temple were stumbled upon, and the inscriptions thereon had to be copied. These were too fragmentary to be of much importance, and, except for the above-mentioned ancient name of Kossair there written, no point of particular interest requires to be noted here. We lunched and dined off the most excellent fish, a species named *belbul* being particularly palatable, while crayfish and a kind of cockles were immoderately indulged in. Having arranged to try our hand at the catching of crayfish during the night hours, we turned in early to sleep for a short time until the fishermen should call us.

The summons having come at about 11 p.m., we set out along the moonlit shore, two fishermen and a boy accompanying us, carrying nets and lanterns. Our destination was a spot at which the coral reefs, projecting into the sea, presented so flat a surface that the incoming tide would wash over the whole area at a depth of not more than a few inches. In the shallow water, we were told, the crayfish would crawl, attracted by our lanterns, and we could then pick them up with our fingers. These crayfish are not at first sight distinguishable from larger lobsters, though a second glance will show that the difference lies in the fact that they have no claws, and therefore can be caught with impunity. They are fearsome -looking creatures, nevertheless, often measuring twenty inches or so from head to tail. In eating them it is hard to believe that one is not eating the most tasty of lobsters.

A tedious walk of over three miles somewhat damped our ardour; and as the fishermen told us that the moon was too high and the tide too low for good hunting, we were not in the best spirits when at last we turned on to the coral reef. Here, however, the scene was so weirdly picturesque that the catching of the crayfish became a matter of secondary import. The surface of the reef, though flat, was broken and jagged, and much seaweed grew upon it. In the uncertain light of the moon it was difficult to walk without stumbling; but the ghostly figures of the fishermen hovered in front of us, and silently led the way out towards the sea, which uttered continuously a kind of sobbing as it washed over the edges of the coral reef. This and the unholy wail of the curlews were the only sounds, for the fishermen had imposed silence upon us, and the moonlight furthered their wishes.

As we walked over the reef we had to pick our way between several small patches of water some five or six feet in breadth, which appeared to be shallow pools left by the last tide in the slight depressions of the rock. Presently one noticed that in these pools white clouds appeared to be reflected from the sky, but quickly looking up one saw that the heavens were cloudless. Staring closer at the water, it suddenly dawned upon one that these white clouds were in reality the sand at the bottom of the pools, and as suddenly came the discovery that the bottom lay at a depth of fifteen feet or more. Now one went on hands and knees to gaze down at those moonlit depths, and one realised

AFRICA

If you pick 'em up, O Lord, I'll put 'em down.
ANON *PRAYER OF THE TIRED WALKER*

that each pool was a great globular cavern, the surface area being but the small mouth of it.

One found oneself kneeling on a projecting ridge of coral which was deeply undermined all round; and, looking down into the bowl, one was reminded of nothing so much as of an aquarium tank seen through glass. In the moonlight the cloudy bottom of the caverns could be discerned, whereon grew great anemones and the fair flowers of the sea. Sometimes an arched gallery, suffused with pale light, led from one cavern to the next, the ceiling of these passages decorated with dim plants, the floor with coloured shells. Not easily could one have been carried so completely into the realms of Fairyland as one was by the gazing at these depths. Presently there sailed through the still water the dim forms of fishes, and now through the galleries there moved two shining lamps, as though carried by the little men of the sea to light them amidst the anemones. Two more small lamps passed into the cavern and floated through the water, now glowing amidst the tendrils of the sea plants, now rising towards the surface, and now sinking again to the shells, the sand, and the flowers at the bottom.

It was not at once that one could bring oneself to realise that these lights were the luminous eyes of a strange fish, the name of which I do not know; but now the fishermen, who had suddenly drawn their net across the edge of the reef and had driven a dozen leaping creatures on to the exposed rock, beckoned us to look at this curious species at close quarters. Their bodies were transparent, and from around their mouths many filmy tentacles waved. The eyes were large and brown in colour, and appeared as fantastic stone orbs set in a glass body. Many other varieties of fish were caught as the tide came in; but it appeared that the moon was too powerful for successful sport in regard to the crayfish, and the catch consisted of but four of these. The sight of the fairy caverns, however, was entertainment sufficient for one night; and it was with discontent that one turned away from these fair kingdoms of the sea to return in the small hours of the morning to the tents. The moonlight, the sobbing of the ocean, the deep caverns lit by unearthly lamps, left an impression of unre-

AFRICA

A line is a dot that went for a walk.
PAUL KLEE

ality upon the mind which it was not easy to dispel; and one felt that a glance had been vouchsafed through the forbidden gates, and a glimpse had been obtained of scenes unthought of since the days of one's childhood. Had we also tasted of the lotos, and was this but one of the dreams of dreamy Kossair?

(From *Travels in the Upper Egyptian Desert*; William Blackwood & Sons, Edinburgh & London, 1913)

Travels in West Africa, 1894

MARY KINGSLEY

Mary Kingsley (1862-1900) made several journeys to Africa in the 1890s, studying zoology and collecting information about African societies. In 1894 she travelled through parts of the Cameroons hitherto unvisited by white men let alone white women. Crossing the territory of the Fan people, she walks on ahead, the path suddenly gives way and she falls into a game pit ...

It is at these times you realise the blessing of a good thick skirt. Had I paid heed to the advice of many people in England, who ought to have known better, and did not do it themselves, and adopted masculine garments, I should have been spiked to the bone, and done for. Whereas, save for a good many bruises, here I was with the fulness of my skirt tucked under me, sitting on nine ebony spikes some twelve inches long, in comparative comfort, howling lustily to be hauled out. The Duke came along first, and looked down at me. I said, 'Get a bush-rope, and haul me out.' He grunted and sat down on a log. The Passenger came next, and he looked down. 'You kill?' says he. 'Not much,' say I; 'get a bush-rope and haul me out.' 'No fit,' says he, and sat down on the log. Presently, however, Kiva and Wiki came up, and Wiki went and selected the one and only bush-rope suitable to haul an English lady, of my exact complexion, age, and size, out of that one particular pit. They seemed rare round there from the time he took; and I was just casting about in my mind as to what method would be best to employ in getting up the smooth, yellow, sandy-clay, incurved walls, when he arrived with it, and I was out in a

Methinks that the moment my legs begin to move, my thoughts begin to flow.
H.D. THOREAU

twinkling, and very much ashamed of myself, until Silence, who was then leading, disappeared through the path before us with a despairing yell. Each man then pulled the skin cover off his gun lock, carefully looked to see if things there were all right and loosened his knife in its snake-skin sheath; and then we set about hauling poor Silence out, binding him up where necessary with cool green leaves; for he, not having a skirt, had got a good deal frayed at the edges on those spikes. Then we closed up, for the Fans said these pits were symptomatic of the immediate neighbourhood of Efoua.

We sounded our ground, as we went into a thick plantain patch, through which we could see a great clearing in the forest, and the low huts of a big town. We charged into it, going right through the guard-house gateway, at one end, in single file, as its narrowness obliged us, and into the street-shaped town, and formed ourselves into as imposing a looking party as possible in the centre of the street.

The Efouerians regarded us with much amazement, and the women and children cleared off into the huts, and took stock of us through the door-holes. There were but few men in the town, the majority, we subsequently learnt, being away after elephants.

☆   ☆   ☆

I shook hands with and thanked the chief, and directed that all the loads should be placed inside the huts. I must admit my good friend was a villainous-looking savage, but he behaved most hospitably and kindly. From what I had heard of the Fan, I deemed it advisable not to make any present to him at once, but to base my claim on him on the right of an amicable stranger to hospitality. When I had seen all the baggage stowed I went outside and sat at the doorway on a rather rickety mushroom-shaped stool in the cool evening air, waiting for my tea which I wanted bitterly. Pagan came up as usual for tobacco to buy chop with; and after giving it to him, I and the two chiefs, with Gray Shirt acting as interpreter, had a long chat. Of course the first question was, Why was I there?

I told them I was on my way to the factory of H. and C. on the Rembwe. They said they had heard of 'Ugumu,' i.e., Messrs

AFRICA

Hatton and Cookson, but they did not trade direct with them, passing their trade into towns nearer to the Rembwe, which were swindling bad towns, they said; and they got the idea stuck in their heads that I was a trader, a sort of bagman for the firm, and Gray Shirt could not get this idea out, so off one of their majesties went and returned with twenty-five balls of rubber, which I bought to promote good feeling, subsequently dashing them to Wiki, who passed them in at Ndorko when we got there. I also bought some elephant-hair necklaces from one of the chiefs' wives, by exchanging my red silk tie with her for them, and one or two other things. I saw fish-hooks would not be of much value because Efoua was not near a big water of any sort; so I held fish-hooks and traded handkerchiefs and knives.

☆　☆　☆

The chiefs made furious raids on the mob of spectators who pressed round the door, and stood with their eyes glued to every crack in the bark of which the hut was made. The next door neighbours on either side might have amassed a comfortable competence for their old age, by letting out seats for the circus. Every hole in the side walls had a human eye in it, and I heard new holes being bored in all directions; so I deeply fear the chief, my host, must have found his palace sadly draughty. I felt perfectly safe and content, however, although Ngouta suggested the charming idea that 'P'r'aps them M'fetta Fan done sell we.' As soon as all my men had come in, and established themselves in the inner room for the night, I curled up among the boxes, with my head on the tobacco sack, and dozed.

After about half an hour I heard a row in the street, and looking out, – for I recognised his grace's voice taking a solo part followed by choruses, – I found him in legal difficulties about a murder case. An alibi was proved for the time being; that is to say the prosecution could not bring up witnesses because of the elephant hunt; and I went in for another doze, and the town at last grew quiet. Waking up again I noticed the smell in the hut was violent, from being shut up I suppose, and it had an unmistakably organic origin. Knocking the ash end off the smouldering bush-light that lay burning on the floor, I investigated, and

In the morning a man walks with his whole body; in the evening, only with his legs. RALPH WALDO EMERSON

AFRICA

tracked it to those bags, so I took down the biggest one, and carefully noted exactly how the tie-tie had been put round its mouth; for these things are important and often mean a lot. I then shook its contents out in my hat, for fear of losing anything of value. They were a human hand, three big toes, four eyes, two ears, and other portions of the human frame. The hand was fresh, the others only so so, and shrivelled.

Replacing them I tied the bag up, and hung it up again. I subsequently learnt that although the Fans will eat their fellow friendly tribesfolk, yet they like to keep a little something belonging to them as a memento. This touching trait in their character I learnt from Wiki; and, though it's to their credit, under the circumstances, still it's an unpleasant practice when they hang the remains in the bedroom you occupy, particularly if the bereavement in your host's family has been recent. I did not venture to prowl round Efoua; but slid the bark door aside and looked out to get a breath of fresh air.

(From *Travels in West Africa*; Macmillan & Co, London, 1897)

A Trek to Mt Elgon, 1925

CARL JUNG

Carl Jung (1875-1961), the Swiss psychiatrist, visited Kenya and Uganda in 1925. He was interested in the myths and religious symbolism of primitive peoples and looking for analogies between them and the unconscious psyche of Western Man.

Next day, with the aid of the D.C., we rounded up our column of bearers, which was supplemented by a military escort of three Askaris. And now began the trek to Mt. Elgon, whose fourteen-thousand-foot crater wall we soon saw on the horizon. The track led through relatively dry savanna covered with umbrella acacias. The whole district was densely covered with small, round tumuli between six and ten feet high – old termite colonies.

For travellers there were rest-houses along the track – round, grass-roofed, rammed-earth huts, open and empty. At night a burning lantern was placed in the entrance as protection against

All truly great thoughts are conceived while walking.
FRIEDRICH NIETZSCHE

intruders. Our cook had no lantern; but as a compensation he had a miniature hut all to himself, with which he was highly pleased. But it nearly proved fatal to him. The previous day he had slaughtered in front of his hut a sheep that we had bought for five Uganda shillings, and had prepared excellent mutton chops for our evening meal. After dinner, while we were sitting around the fire, smoking, we heard strange noises in the distance. The sounds came closer. They sounded now like the growling of bears, now like the barking and yapping of dogs; then again the sounds became shrill, like shrieks and hysterical laughter. My first impression was: This is like a comic turn at Barnum and Bailey's. Before long, however, the scene became more menacing: we were surrounded on all sides by a huge pack of hungry hyenas who had obviously smelled the sheep's blood. They performed an infernal concert, and in the glow of the fire their eyes could be seen glittering from the tall elephant grass.

In spite of our lofty knowledge of the nature of hyenas, which are alleged not to attack man, we did not feel altogether sure of ourselves and suddenly a frightful human scream came from behind the rest-house. We snatched up our arms (a 9mm. Mannlicher rifle and a shotgun) and fired several rounds in the direction of those glittering lights. As we did so, our cook came rushing panic-stricken into our midst and babbled that a *fizi* (hyena) had come into his hut and almost killed him. The whole camp was in an uproar. The excitement, it seemed, so frightened the pack of hyenas that they quit the scene, protesting noisily. The bearers went on laughing for a long time, after which the rest of the night passed quietly, without further disturbance. Early next morning the local chief appeared with a gift of two chickens and a basketful of eggs. He implored us to stay another day to shoot the hyenas. The day before, he said, they had dragged out an old man asleep in his hut and eaten him. *De Africa nihil certum*!

At daybreak roars of laughter began again in the boys' quarters. It appeared that they were re-enacting the events of the night. One of them played the sleeping cook, and one of the soldiers played the creeping hyena, approaching the sleeper with

I cannot walk through the suburbs in the solitude of the night without thinking that the night pleases us because it suppresses idle details, just as memory does. JORGE LUIS BORGES

murderous intent. This playlet was repeated I don't know how many times, to the utter delight of the audience.

☆　☆　☆

The terrain sloped gently upwards. Signs of Tertiary lava beds increased. We passed through glorious stretches of jungle with huge Nandi flame trees flaunting their red blossoms. Enormous beetles and even larger brilliantly coloured butterflies enlivened the clearings and the edges of the jungle. Branches were shaken by inquisitive monkeys as we advanced farther into the bush. It was a paradisial world. For most of the way we still traversed flat savanna with deep red soil. We tramped mostly along the native trails which meandered in strikingly sharp turns. Our route led us into the Nandi region, and through the Nandi Forest, a sizable area of jungle. Without incident we reached a rest·house at the foot of Mt. Elgon, which had been towering higher and higher above our heads for days. Here the climb began, along a narrow path. We were greeted by the local chief, who was the son of the *laibon*, the medicine man. He rode a pony – the only horse we had seen. From him we learned that his tribe belonged to the Masai, but lived in isolation here on the slopes of Mt. Elgon.

☆　☆　☆

The sunrise in these latitudes was a phenomenon that over-whelmed me anew every day. The drama of it lay less in the splendour of the sun's shooting up over the horizon than in what happened afterwards. I formed the habit of taking my camp stool and sitting under an umbrella acacia just before dawn. Before me, at the bottom of the little valley, lay a dark, almost black-green strip of jungle, with the rim of the plateau on the opposite side of the valley towering above it. At first, the contrasts between light and darkness would be extremely sharp. Then objects would assume contour and emerge into the light which seemed to fill the valley with a compact brightness. The horizon above became radiantly white. Gradually the swelling light seemed to penetrate into the very structure of objects, which became illuminated from within until at last they shone translucently, like bits of coloured glass. Everything turned to

AFRICA

Truly it may be said that the outside of a mountain is good for the inside of a man.
GEORGE WHERRY

flaming crystal. The cry of the bell bird rang round the horizon. At such moments I felt as if I were inside a temple. It was the most sacred hour of the day. I drank in this glory with insatiable delight, or rather, in a timeless ecstasy.

Near my observation point was a high cliff inhabited by big baboons. Every morning they sat quietly, almost motionless, on the ridge of the cliff facing the sun, whereas throughout the rest of the day they ranged noisily through the forest, screeching and chattering. Like me, they seemed to be waiting for the sunrise. They reminded me of the great baboons of the temple of Abu Simbel in Egypt, which perform the gesture of adoration. They tell the same story: for untold ages men have worshipped the great god who redeems the world by rising out of the darkness as a radiant light in the heavens.

(From *Memories, Dreams, Reflections*, translated from the German by Richard and Clara Winston; Collins and Routledge & Kegan Paul, London, 1963)

Victoria Falls, 1874

FRANK OATES

Naturalist Frank Oates (1840–1875), uncle of the more famous Arctic explorer Laurence Oates, was one of the first Europeans to see Metse-a-tunya, the waterfalls that are now better known as Victoria Falls. He died a month later on the way home and his letters were collected into a book by his brother, Charles.

Pantamatenka, December 27th, 1874. — I am just about to set off, to walk to the Victoria Falls, which are only three days from here. This place is somewhere about fifteen miles to the north-westward of Daka, a place you will probably see in any recent map. Neither place is a town of any sort, but each is merely a river flowing to the Zambesi. At both rivers waggons stand, as they are both out of 'the fly.' The place where I now am is quite civilized, as it is a trading-station, and the man in charge here has a snug little house, well thatched, to keep out the rain. He has lived here three years, and is in the employ of Westbeach, who is at present at the residence of Sepopo, the Zambesi chief, some distance up

Doomed for a certain term to walk at night.
WILLIAM SHAKESPEARE, *HAMLET*

the river. His man, Blockley, undertakes the charge of my effects whilst I proceed to the Falls.

☆   ☆   ☆

There was a grand plum-pudding made here on Christmas Day. Besides Blockley and the doctor there are two traders, who arrived here after I did, on their way from the Zambesi. One has been ill and the doctor prohibited him plum-pudding, so there were four of us in all. We ate nothing but pudding on Christmas Day and the day following, with scarcely an exception. The men had another pudding. My man turns out to have been originally a cook, and when he likes can cook well. The doctor was found to be five pounds heavier after dinner than before it on Christmas Day. He strongly urged upon all of us the desirability of moderation, but no one seemed to pay much attention to him, and he certainly did not practise what he preached. He has been to the Falls before, and in the rainy season too, so he knows what he is undertaking in going with me. I expect he will make very slow marches, but so much the better. I am going to take with me the identical tent I had with me in America, and which proved so effectual a shelter from the snows of the Rocky Mountains. There was a grand idea in the doctor's mind of taking a lot of cold plum-pudding with us on our walk, but the last morsel disappeared last night. However, we shall not be badly off for supplies.

☆   ☆   ☆

One of my goats was reported to have been killed by a leopard on Christmas Eve. We all went with our guns, and I took my dogs. We found the unfortunate goat lying dead, a live companion standing over it ; and, also standing over it, and facing the live goat, an animal I thought was a dog. They told me it was the leopard, but I would not fire, still thinking it a dog. At last, however, I saw what it was, and we shot it. Two others ran away, and my dogs killed both of them gallantly, and in next to no time. They were cheetahs, a sort of leopard, very lanky, and a good deal like greyhounds in appearance. They were very thin, and probably very hungry when they killed the goat ; but the other goat must have kept them from eating it, as it had been killed a considerable time when we got to it.

AFRICA

I walked barefoot – the only way to walk on a muddy road.
LAURIE GOUGH, *LIGHT ON A MOONLESS NIGHT*

I must now get up and make ready to start. I am writing in the tent, having had a cup of coffee as usual, but not got up yet. I intended to have written this letter last night, and, having failed to do so, thought it best to make sure of its being written before I began anything else.

I hope you are all spending a pleasant Christmas and New Year's time at home, or wherever you are ; and wish every one a very happy New Year.

December 27th. — Fine hot day, with a north-easterly breeze. As my own boys had all requested to accompany me, wishing to see 'Metse-a-tunya,' I took all (eight in number) except the Bushman, whom, with two Makalakas engaged for me at Pantamatenka ... and left the Pantamatenka a little before sun-down; walked three miles up the river, and, crossing it, encamped for the night. During the walk I saw a fine tall palm – the first tall one I have seen. The leaves were fan-like and the tree extremely graceful.

☆　☆　☆

December 29th. — Fine morning, but rather cloudy ; a few drops of rain in the afternoon. Had coffee, and again started early. Immediately after starting crossed another stream, also running, they say, into the Pantamatenka. Giraffe and quagga spoor seen. We only went six miles to-day, as one of the boys had to be sent back for an axe, and we waited for him. Mackenna, who had gone on alone, presently returned, having shot two rhinoceros, and we all went to the place and camped there.

December 30th. — Cloudy; a shower in the afternoon. Walked ten miles to-day, crossing at least two sandbelts, the last of which was stony, and with a very thin stratum of soil on it ; the trees few and sparsely scattered. Some dry stony spruits here, and a fine view of the opposite sandbelt. Slept at a spruit in the hollow beneath us, where we had stopped to make tea in the afternoon, but where it looked so threatening we had pitched the tent. However, the rain was trifling. Some of Tibakai's Bushmen were seen and talked to. Whilst the boys were making the huts, they pointed out the cloud on the horizon to the northward from Metse-a-tunya. It keeps rising in a white puff, and passing away in

AFRICA

There ain't no surer way to find out whether you like people or hate them than to travel with them. MARK TWAIN

little fleecy clouds. The others heard the Falls; I am not sure I did.

December 31st. — Rather cloudy; heavy rain about sundown. Fine night. Went, roughly, say three miles further north across turf, to the river where I thought Tibakai was encamped, but found we were too much to the left, so after crossing the river kept down it about three-quarters of a mile to his camp. ... I left the boys and traps under a tree amongst the huts, and went with the doctor and John to have an interview with Tibakai. He is a Mungwato headman, with one or two of his own people, but all the rest are Bushmen, hunting for him, and staying with him with their families. Tibakai said we could not go to the Falls – he was captain here. Hearing, however, we did not come to hunt, he said we might go but must make our scherm here, and stay till to-morrow, when we might visit the Falls and return. He then conceded that we might have two Bushmen, whom he would give us to-night when they returned from hunting, but said we *must* sleep here to-night. I said we must go, and he could do as he pleased about the Bushmen. After this he again said we must stay to-night. This I flatly refused to do, and had already told him we should shoot elephants if we saw them. John wanted me to stay, and refused to come away. I ordered the boys to start, they having already told me they were willing, and again for the third time called John. We then started, all but him, and there was a great stir in the place ; caps snapping, and one fellow running out with his gun. We moved on, I on the flank ready to fire; but it was not necessary. John remained behind, but, seeing us get away, joined us, and, when I upbraided him, said he was only waiting to see what they would do.'

☆ ☆ ☆

[**Charles Oates continues** ...] And now a walk of some twelve or fifteen miles brought them to the goal. The latter part – five miles or so – of this was over rolling ground, and here, as they advanced, they soon began to see more clearly the distant clouds of vapour from the Falls, and hear them more distinctly. The trees, before thinly scattered, were now fine and close together, and for a time obscured the view. Then shortly, through an open-

AFRICA

One's destination is never a place, but a new way of seeing things. HENRY MILLER

ing in their midst, the columns of spray again were visible, now quite near, and the party pressed quickly on. The sun was about to set, and clouds were gathering, as if for an approaching storm. Stopping to shelter from a heavy shower just above the river, the first sight of *Metse-a-tunya* was here caught through the trees, and a halt was ordered for the night.

Thus, the last day of 1874, the sun set on the fulfilment – after many hindrances – of the traveller's great desire!

(From *Matabele land and the Victoria Falls*;
Kegan Paul, London, 1881)

Climbing Mt Cameroon, 1895

MARY KINGSLEY

Undeterred by the weather, Mary Kingsley (1862-1900) climbs 'The Great Peak of Cameroons: Mungo Mah Lobeh' (Mt Cameroon, 4,040m).

September 26th. – The weather is undecided and so am I, for I feel doubtful about going on in this weather, but I do not like to give up the peak after going through so much for it. The boys being dry and warm with the fires have forgotten their troubles. However, I settle in my mind to keep on, and ask for volunteers to come with me, and Bum, the Head man, and Xenia announce their willingness.

I put two tins of meat and a bottle of Herr Liebert's beer into the little wooden box, and insist on both men taking a blanket apiece, much to their disgust, and before six o'clock we are off over the crater plain. It is a broken bit of country with rock mounds sparsely overgrown with tufts of grass, and here and there are patches of boggy land, not real bog, but damp places where grow little clumps of rushes, and here and there among the rocks sorely-afflicted shrubs of broom, and the yellow-flowered shrub I have mentioned before, and quantities of very sticky heather, feeling when you catch hold of it as if it had been covered with syrup. One might fancy the entire race of shrubs was dying out; for one you see partially alive there are twenty skeletons which fall to pieces as you brush past them.

Backpacking is an extended form of hiking in which people carry double the amount of gear they need for half the

☆   ☆   ☆

We keep as straight as we can, but get driven at an angle by the strange ribs of rock which come straight down. These are most tiresome to deal with, getting worse the higher we go, and so rotten and weather-eaten are they that they crumble into dust and fragments under our feet. Head man gets half a dozen falls, and when we are about three parts of the way up Xenia gives in. The cold and the climbing are too much for him, so I make him wrap himself up in his blanket, which he is glad enough of now, and shelter in a depression under one of the many rock ridges, and Head man and I go on.

When we are some 600 feet higher the iron-grey mist comes curling and waving round the rocks above us, like some savage monster defending them from intruders, and I again debate whether I was justified in risking the men, for it is a risk for them at this low temperature, with the evil weather I know, and they do not know, is coming on. But still we have food and blankets with us enough for them, and the camp in the plain below they can reach all right, if the worst comes to the worst; and for myself – well – that's my own affair, and no one will be a ha'porth the worse if I am dead in an hour. So I hitch myself on to the rocks, and take bearings, particularly bearings of Xenia's position, who, I should say, has got a tin of meat and a flask of rum with him, and then turn and face the threatening mist. It rises and falls, and sends out arm-like streams towards us, and then Bum, the Head man, decides to fail for the third time to reach the peak, and I leave him wrapped in his blanket with the bag of provisions, and go on alone into the wild, grey, shifting, whirling mist above, and soon find myself at the head of a rock ridge in a narrowish depression, walled by massive black walls which show fitfully but firmly through the mist.

I can see three distinctly high cones before me, and then the mist, finding it cannot drive me back easily, proceeds to desperate methods, and lashes out with a burst of bitter wind, and a sheet of blinding, stinging rain. I make my way up through it towards a peak which I soon see through a tear in the mist is not the highest, so I angle off and go up the one to the left, and after

AFRICA

a desperate fight reach the cairn – only, alas! to find a hurricane raging and a fog in full possession, and not a ten yards' view to be had in any direction. Near the cairn on the ground are several bottles, some of which the energetic German officers, I suppose, had emptied in honour of their achievement, an achievement I bow down before, for their pluck and strength had taken them here in a shorter time by far than mine. I do not meddle with anything, save to take a few specimens and to put a few more rocks on the cairn, and to put in among them my card, merely as a civility to Mungo, a civility his Majesty will soon turn into pulp. Not that it matters – what is done is done.

The weather grows worse every minute, and no sign of any clearing shows in the indigo sky or the wind-reft mist. The rain lashes so fiercely I cannot turn my face to it and breathe, the wind is all I can do to stand up against.

Verily I am no mountaineer, for there is in me no exultation, but only a deep disgust because the weather has robbed me of my main object in coming here, namely to get a good view and an idea of the way the unexplored mountain range behind Calabar trends. I took my chance and it failed, so there's nothing to complain about.

(From *Travels in West Africa*; Macmillan & Co, London, 1897)

Visiting the Cango Caves, 1877
ANTHONY TROLLOPE

The novelist Anthony Trollope (1815-82) travelled around South Africa in 1877. He describes his visit to these caverns, now a popular tourist site near Oudtshoorn in the Western Cape province.

I have made my way into various underground halls, the mansions of bats and stalactites. Those near Deloraine in Tasmania are by far the most spacious in ascertained length that I have seen. Those at Wonderfontein in the Transvaal, of which I will speak in the next volume, may be, and probably are, larger still, but they have never been explored. In both of these the stalactites are much poorer in form than in the caves of the Cheddar cliffs, – which however are comparatively small. The Mammoth Caves in

Thoughts come clearly while one walks.
THOMAS MANN

Kentucky I have not visited; but I do not understand that the sub-terranean formations are peculiarly grand. In the Cango Grottoes the chambers are very much bigger than in the Tasmanian Caves. They also have not been fully explored. But the wonderful forms and vagaries of the stalactites are infinitely finer than anything I have seen elsewhere.

We brought with us many blue lights, – a sort of luminary which spreads a powerful glare to a considerable distance for three or four minutes, – without which it would be impossible to see the shapes around. The candles which we carried with us for our own guidance had little or no effect.

In some places the droppings had assumed the shape of falling curtains. Across the whole side of a hall, perhaps sixty feet long, these would hang in regular pendent drapery, fold upon fold, seeming to be as equal and regular as might be the heavy folds protecting some inner sacred chapel. And in the middle of the folds there would be the entrance, through which priests and choristers and people might walk as soon as the machinery had been put to work and the curtain had been withdrawn. In other places there would hang from the roof the collected gathered pleats, all regular, as though the machinery had been at work. Here there was a huge organ with its pipes, and some grotesque figure at the top of it as though the constructor of all these things had feared no raillery. In other places there were harps against the walls, from which, as the blue lights burned, one expected to hear sounds of perhaps not celestial minstrelsy. And pillars were erected up to the ceiling, – not a low grovelling ceiling against which the timid visitor might fear to strike his head, but a noble roof, perfected, groined, high up, as should be that of a noble hall. That the columns had in fact come drop by drop from the rock above us did not alter their appearance. There was one very thick, of various shapes, grotesque and daring, looking as though the base were some wondrous animal of hideous form that had been made to bear the superstructure from age to age. Then as the eye would struggle to examine it upwards, and to divide the details each from the others, the blue light would go out and the mystery would remain. Another blue light would be made to burn; but

AFRICA

When people start talking of man's inhumanity to man it probably means they haven't actually walked far enough.
BRUCE CHATWIN

bats would come flitting through, disturbing all investigation; –
and the mystery would still remain.

There were various of these halls or chambers, all opening
one to another by passages here and there, so that the visitor who
is never compelled to travel far, might suppose them all to be
parts of one huge dark mansion underground. But in each hall
there were receding closets, guarded by jutting walls of stalactite
breast high, round which however on closer search, a way would
be found, – as though these might be the private rooms in which
the ghouls would hide themselves when thus disturbed by footsteps and voices, by candles and blue lights from above. I was
always thinking that I should come upon a ghoul; but there were
inner chambers still into which they crept, and whither I could
not follow them.

Careful walking is necessary, as the ground is uneven; and
there are places in which the ghouls keep their supply of water, –
stone troughs wonderfully and beautifully made, but except in
one place there is no real difficulty in moving about, when once
the visitor to the Caves has descended into them. At this place the
ascent is perplexing, because the ground is both steep and slippery. I can imagine that a lady or an old man might find it difficult
to be dragged up. Such lady or old man should either remain
below or allow his companions to drag him up. There is very little
stooping necessary anywhere. But it has to be borne in mind that
after entering the mouth of the cave and reaching the first chamber, the realms I have described have to be reached by an iron ladder which holds 38 steps. To get on to this ladder requires some little care and perhaps a dash of courage. The precautions taken,
however, suffice, and I think I may say that there is no real danger.

We called at a Dutch Boer's house about a mile from the
Caves, and were accompanied by three members of the Boer's
family. This is usual, and, I believe, absolutely necessary. I paid
one of the men a sovereign for his trouble, – which sum he named
as his regular price for the assistance provided. He found the candles, but some of our party took the blue lights with them.
Nothing could have been seen without them.

(From *South Africa*, Volume 1; Chapman and Hall, London, 1878)

The end is where we start from.
T.S. ELIOT, *FOUR QUARTETS*

AUSTRALASIA

7

The Songlines, 1987

BRUCE CHATWIN

My reason for coming to Australia was to try to learn for myself, and not from other men's books, what a Songline was – and how it worked. Obviously, I was not going to get to the heart of the matter, nor would I want to. I had asked a friend in Adelaide if she knew of an expert. She gave me Arkady's phone number.

'Do you mind if I use my notebook?' I asked.

'Go ahead'.

I pulled from my pocket a black, oilcloth-covered notebook, its pages held in place with an elastic band.

'Nice notebook,' he said.

'I used to get them in Paris,' I said. 'But now they don't make them any more.'

'Paris?' he repeated, raising an eyebrow as if he'd never heard anything so pretentious.

Then he winked and went on talking.

To get to grips with the concept of the Dreamtime, he said, you had to understand it as an Aboriginal equivalent of the first two chapters of Genesis – with one significant difference.

In Genesis, God first created the 'living things' then fashioned Father Adam from clay. Here in Australia, the Ancestors created themselves from clay, hundreds and thousands of them, one for each totemic species.

'So when an Aboriginal tells you, "I have a Wallaby Dreaming," he means, "My totem is Wallaby. I am a member of the Wallaby Clan"'.

'So a Dreaming is a clan emblem? A badge to distinguish "us" from "them"? "Our country" from "their country"?'

'Much more than that,' he said.

Every Wallaby Man believed he was descended

from a universal Wallaby Father, who was the ancestor of all other Wallaby Men and all living wallabies. Wallabies, therefore, were his brothers. To kill one for food was both fratricide and cannibalism.

'Yet,' I persisted, 'the man was no more wallaby than the British are lions, the Russians bears, or the Americans bald eagles?'

'Any species', he said 'can be a Dreaming. A virus can be a Dreaming. You can have a chickenpox Dreaming, a rain Dreaming, a desert-orange Dreaming, a lice dreaming. In the Kimberleys they've now got a money Dreaming.'

'And the Welsh have leeks, the Scots thistles and Daphne was changed into a laurel.'

'Same old story,' he said.

He went on to explain how each totemic ancestor, while travelling through the country, was thought to have scattered a trail of words and musical notes along the line of his footprints, and how these Dreaming-tracks lay over the land as 'ways' of communication between the most far-flung tribes.

'A song,' he said, 'was both map and direction-finder. Providing you knew the song, you could always find your way across country.'

'And would a man on "Walkabout" always be travelling down one of the Songlines?'

'In the old days, yes,' he agreed. 'Nowadays, they go by train or car.'

'Suppose the man strayed from his Songline?'

'He was trespassing. He might get speared for it.'

'But as long as he stuck to the track, he'd always find people who shared his Dreaming? Who were, in fact, his brothers?'

'Yes.'

'From whom he could expect hospitality?'

'And vice versa.'

'So song is a kind of passport and meal-ticket?'

'Again, it's more complicated.'

In theory, at least, the whole of Australia could be read as a musical score. There was hardly a rock or creek in the country

Walking is a virtue, tourism is a deadly sin.
BRUCE CHATWIN, *WHAT AM I DOING HERE?*

that could not or had not been sung. One should perhaps visualize the Songlines as a spaghetti of Iliads and Odysseys, writhing this way and that, in which every 'episode' was readable in terms of geology.

(From *The Songlines*; Jonathan Cape, London, 1987, © Bruce Chatwin)

The Duck and the Kangaroo, 1871
EDWARD LEAR

Although Edward Lear (1812-88) was also an accomplished painter and musician, it is for his limericks and other humorous verse that he is chiefly remembered.

Said the Duck to the Kangaroo,
 'Good gracious! how you hop
Over the fields and the water too,
 As if you never would stop!

My life is a bore in this nasty pond,
And I long to go out in the world beyond!
 I wish I could hop like you!'
 Said the Duck to the Kangaroo.

'Please give me a ride on your back!'
 Said the Duck to the Kangaroo.
'I would sit quite still, and say nothing but 'Quack,'
 The whole of the long day through!

And we'd go to the Dee, and the Jelly Bo Lee,
Over the land, and over the sea; –
 Please take me a ride! O do!'
 Said the Duck to the Kangaroo.

Said the Kangaroo to the Duck,
 'This requires some little reflection;
Perhaps on the whole it might bring me luck,
 And there seems but one objection,

Take a walk on the wild side.
LOU REED & NELSON ALGREN

Which is, if you'll let me speak so bold,
Your feet are unpleasantly wet and cold,
And would probably give me the roo-
    Matiz!' said the Kangaroo.

Said the Duck, 'As I sate on the rocks,
    I have thought over that completely,
And I bought four pairs of worsted socks
    Which fit my web-feet neatly

And to keep out the cold I've bought a cloak,
And every day a cigar I'll smoke,
    All to follow my own dear true
    Love of a Kangaroo!'

Said the Kangaroo, 'I'm ready!
    All in the moonlight pale;
But to balance me well, dear Duck, sit steady!
    And quite at the end of my tail!'

So away they went with a hop and a bound,
And they hopped the whole world three times round;
    And who so happy, – O who,
    As the Duck and the Kangaroo?

(From *Lear's Nonsense Drolleries*; Frederick Warne and Co, London, 1889)

The only exercise I take is walking behind the coffins of friends who took exercise. PETER O'TOOLE

BIBLIOGRAPHY

Alcock, Thomas *Travels in Russia, Persia, Turkey, and Greece, in 1828-9,* (1831)

Austen, Jane *Pride and Prejudice* (T. Egerton, London, 1813)

Bates, Henry Walter *The Naturalist on the River Amazons* (John Murray, London, 1863)

Belloc, Hilaire *The Path to Rome* (George Allen, London, 1902)

Bird, Isabella *A Lady's Life in the Rocky Mountains* (GP Putnam's Sons, 1886)

Bird, Isabella *Among the Tibetans* (Revell, New York, 1894)

Bryson, Bill *The Road to Little Dribbling – More Notes from a Small Island* (Doubleday, Transworld, London, 2015)

Chatwin, Bruce *Anatomy of Restlessness: Selected Writings, 1969-1989* (Jonathan Cape, London, 1997)

Chatwin, Bruce *The Songlines* (Jonathan Cape, London, 1987)

Chesterton, G.K. *The Collected Poems of G. K. Chesterton* (1927)

Clare, John *Poems Chiefly from Manuscript* (Cobden-Sanderson, London, 1920)

Dickens, Charles *The Uncommercial Traveller* (1861)

Forster, E.M. *A Passage to India* (Edward Arnold (London) & Harcourt Brace (New York), 1924)

Frost, Robert *Mountain Interval* (Henry Holt, New York, 1916)

Gandhi, Mahatma *Young India,* 12-3-1930 and the manuscript of Mahadev Desai's Diary, both in *The Collected Works of Mahatma Gandhi,* (Vol XLIII)

Gibbons, Stella *Cold Comfort Farm* (Longmans, 1932)

Graham, Stephen *A vagabond in the Caucasus, with some notes of his experiences among the Russians* (John Lane, London & New York, 1911)

Hardy, Thomas *Tess of the d'Urbervilles: A Pure Woman* (Macmillan, London, 1891)

Hartley, L.P. *The Go-Between* (Hamish Hamilton, 1953)

Hazlitt, William *William Hazlitt, Selections from his Writings* (Frederick Warne & Co, London, 1889)

Hunt, John *The Ascent of Everest* (Hodder & Stoughton, London, 1953)

Jung, Carl *Memories, Dreams, Reflections,* translated from the German by Richard & Clara Winston (Collins and Routledge & Kegan Paul, London, 1963)

Kierkegaard, Søren *Søren Kierkegaard,* from a letter to Henriette Kierkegaard, (1847)

Kingsley, Mary *Travels in West Africa* (Macmillan & Co, London, 1897)

Lear, Edward *Nonsense Songs, Stories, Botany and Alphabets* (RJ Bush, London, 1871)

Lear, Edward *Lear's Nonsense Drolleries* (Frederick Warne and Co, London, 1889)

Lee, Laurie *As I Walked Out One Midsummer Morning* (André Deutsch, London (Atheneum, New York: 1969)

Leigh Fermor, Patrick *A Time of Gifts – On Foot to Constantinople: from the Hook of Holland to the Middle Danube* (John Murray, London, 1977)

Longfellow, Henry Wadsworth *Supplement to the Courant, Connecticut Courant, Vol VII No 2, Jan 22,* (1842)

Macfarlane, Robert *The Old Ways – A Journey on Foot* (Hamish Hamilton, London, 2012)

Martin, Frederick *The Life of John Clare* (Macmillan & Co, London, 1865)

Moritz, Karl *Travels, chiefly on foot, through several parts of England in 1782, described in Letters to a Friend* (trans 1795)

Murphy, Dervla *Silverland – A Winter Journey Beyond the Urals* (John Murray, London, 2007)

Neruda, Pablo *The Ritual of My Legs (Ritual de mis piernas),* (1931)

Oates, Frank *Matabele land and the Victoria Falls* (Kegan Paul, London, 1881)

Raleigh, Walter *Sir Walter Raleigh (1554–1618) Poems,* 1892)

Rossetti, Christina *Macmillan's Magazine* (February 1861)

Rousseau, Jean Jacques *Confessions* (Aldus Society, London, 1903)

Stanley, Arthur *The Bedside Book* (Victor Gollancz, 1934)

Stevenson, Robert Louis *Walking Tours* published in *Virginibus Puerisque and other papers* (C. Kegan Paul, London, 1881)

Taylor, Bayard *A visit to India, China, and Japan in the year 1853* (G.P. Putnam, New York, 1855)

Taylor, Bayard *Views A-Foot (Europe Seen with Knapsack and Staff* (Wiley & Putnam, New York, 1846)

Thomas, Edward *Poems* (Selwyn & Blount, London, 1917)

Thomson, Rev W.M. *The Land and the Book* (Harper & Bros, New York, 1859)

Thoreau, Henry David *Walking,* published in *Atlantic Monthly* (Boston, 1862)

Townsend, Chris *The Advanced Backpacker: A Handbook of Year-Round Long-Distance Hiking* (Ragged Mountain Press, McGraw Hill, Camden, 2000)

Traherne, Thomas *The Poetical Works of Thomas Traherne* (Dobell, London, 1903)

Trollope, Anthony *Phineas Finn – The Irish Member* (Virtue & Co, London, 1869)

Trollope, Anthony *South Africa,* Volume 1 (Chapman and Hall, London, 1878)

Twain, Mark *A Tramp Abroad* (American Publishing Co, Hartford, Conn, 1880)

Weigall, Arthur E.P. *Travels in the Upper Egyptian Desert* (William Blackwood & Sons, Edinburgh & London, 1913)

White, Gilbert *The Natural History of Selborne* (T. Bensley for B. White & Son, London, 1789)

Whymper, Edward *Travels Amongst the Great Andes of the Equator* (John Murray, London, 1892)

Wordsworth, Dorothy *Journals,* (1800)

Wordsworth, William *William Wordsworth – Poems,* (1845)

TRAILBLAZER TITLE LIST

Adventure Cycle-Touring Handbook
Adventure Motorcycling Handbook
Australia by Rail
Azerbaijan
Coast to Coast (British Walking Guide)
Cornwall Coast Path (British Walking Guide)
Corsica Trekking – GR20
Cotswold Way (British Walking Guide)
The Cyclist's Anthology
Dales Way (British Walking Guide)
Dorset & Sth Devon Coast Path (British Walking Gde)
Exmoor & Nth Devon Coast Path (British Walking Gde)
Great Glen Way (British Walking Guide) – due early 2017
Hadrian's Wall Path (British Walking Guide)
Himalaya by Bike – a route and planning guide
Inca Trail, Cusco & Machu Picchu
Japan by Rail
Kilimanjaro – the trekking guide (includes Mt Meru)
Moroccan Atlas – The Trekking Guide
Morocco Overland (4WD/motorcycle/mountainbike)
Nepal Trekking & The Great Himalaya Trail
New Zealand – The Great Walks
Offa's Dyke Path (British Walking Guide)
Overlanders' Handbook – worldwide driving guide
Peddars Way & Norfolk Coast Path (British Walking Gde)
Pembrokeshire Coast Path (British Walking Guide)
Pennine Way (British Walking Guide)
Peru's Cordilleras Blanca & Huayhuash – Hiking/Biking
The Railway Anthology
The Ridgeway (British Walking Guide)
Sahara Overland – a route and planning guide
Scottish Highlands – The Hillwalking Guide
Siberian BAM Guide – rail, rivers & road
The Silk Roads – a route and planning guide
Sinai – the trekking guide
South Downs Way (British Walking Guide)
Thames Path (British Walking Guide)
Tour du Mont Blanc
Trans-Canada Rail Guide
Trans-Siberian Handbook
Trekking in the Everest Region
The Walker's Anthology
The Walker's Anthology – further tales
The Walker's Haute Route – Mont Blanc to Matterhorn
West Highland Way (British Walking Guide)

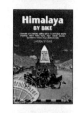

For more information about Trailblazer and our
expanding range of guides, for guidebook updates or
for credit card mail order sales visit our website:

www.trailblazer-guides.com

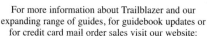

INDEX